#88-2642

creative woodc

E DUE

Techniques of Creative
Woodcarving

Techniques of Creative Woodcarving

Ian Norbury

CHARLES SCRIBNER'S SONS
NEW YORK

First United States edition published by Charles Scribner's Sons 1984
Copyright © 1983 Ian Norbury

Library of Congress Cataloging in Publication Data

Norbury, Ian
    Techniques of creative woodcarving.

    Bibliography: p.
    Includes index.
    1. Wood-carving — Technique. I. Title.
NK9704.N67   1984   731.4′62   84-14011
ISBN 0-684-18210-6

For Malcolm Winlow

without whose
enthusiastic support
this book
would not have
been possible

Acknowledgements

I would like to acknowledge Ken and Pat Ilott for their help and photographic expertise; Tony Walker of Bahco-Record and Mr D. L. Jenner of Massey Wykham for illustrations of tools; Mr D. C. C. Wilson, Miss J. A. Craft, Mr & Mrs P. K. Collier, Mr & Mrs E. Hubar, Mr & Mrs R. Vanden Bosch, Mr & Mrs D. Johnson and Mr & Mrs A. Mitchell for permitting their sculptures to be illustrated. Special thanks also are due to my wife Betty for the many hours of typing and organisation.

Contents

Projects Section

1 Approach to Design

THE post-war British public have witnessed the senility of a patriarch of the arts. With the typical lack of interest we afford to the aged, we have watched the immeasurably ancient craft of woodcarving lapse into meaningless ramblings and repetitions of its youth, turned our backs as some of the finest exponents of the arts churned out pathetic pieces of junk called "repros" for pennies, and muttered about economic viability when cries for help were heard. With monumental hypocrisy the deceased is mourned and legends are created about the miracles that were wrought in days gone by.

The old trade of woodcarving is dead, even if the body is still kicking. There are still many woodcarvers working in this country some of them brilliant technicians; they restore furniture, make copies of antiques, carve memorials, do church-work and so on, but there really is no contemporary style of woodcarving and very little demand for it. It is said that the reason for this is that modern architecture and furniture does not lend itself to decorative carving, but would not the same thing have been said of wrought ironwork or stained glass if they had not been kept alive? Woodcarving was fairly healthy immediately before the war and in a style suited to contemporary taste, however tasteless we may feel it today. The tradition was broken by the war. To quote Peter Morton in *The Woodcarvers Companion* "Where the workshop stood, now there is the factory, where one piece was made now a thousand are made". That was written in the 'fifties and the situation has since hardened and consolidated itself. Woodcarving now occupies a similar position to wheel-wrighting—it still exists and there is no reason why horse drawn vehicles should not be used extensively—but they won't be.

So what is the contemporary situation in the field of woodcarving in Britain? If we discount imitation of antiques in its various manifestations what are we left with? Inevitably, there is the occasional innovator, man of insight, genius or madness who has picked up the severed ends and re-threaded them to create a novel and individual style which could be successor to the old traditions, but there is no sign of it. Indeed, modern furniture makers seem to be casting about in desperation for some obscure predecessor to grub up from the museum vaults and make pieces "inspired by", but the bulk of the good work being done today can be generally put under the heading of Wood Sculpture not Wood-carving.

The modern furniture maker working in his own workshop, creating his own individual pieces to his own design has little in common with the furniture maker of the past who invariably made pieces designed by someone else and worked on by several craftsmen. The craftsman furniture maker is also an artist and a designer, something very few woodcarvers of the past could have called themselves.

The shapes that are designed into much contemporary furniture, no doubt as a reaction against the factory-made product of the last 30 years, frequently involves contours that are too complex or irregular for standard machinery to form, and since they are by definition "one off" the vast expense of making a machine to do the work cannot be contemplated. Added to this is the fact that, as Krenov points out, the importance of the finished piece is giving way, to some extent, to the means by which it was achieved. That is to say that an object made with a hand tool is preferred to one made on a machine, although it may not be as good. How far this philosophy is to be upheld is very unclear, and which machines are acceptable and which are not seems to be a subject best left to the conscience of the craftsmen. However, the fact is, that in the absence of a suitable machine to form an irregular shape the craftsman may resort to hand shaping tools in the forms of spokeshave, scraper, rasp, file, plane, adze, axes and carving tools exclusively for the purpose; but he could hardly be justified in calling himself a woodcarver or the table for example, carved. There is no intention here to start an argument over words, merely to make the point that there is a world of difference between using carving tools as an incidental factor in the creation of an object, and woodcarving as it is understood in the light of tradition.

Similarly, the artist who created a decorative panel, figure or other object, which we would normally call sculpture, but is referred to as woodcarving, is not the legitimate descendant of the man who carved the figures of saints in the gothic cathedrals or the caryatides on the Victorian fire surround. He is primarily a sculptor, creating a three-dimensional form in a rigid material which happens to be wood. The best means available to sculpture wood is to use the tools of the woodcarver. The man who makes bronze figures creates in metal; he is not a metal worker, nor a bronze caster; the material he usually works with is clay or wax but he is not a wax modeller or a clay modeller, but a sculptor. The modern wood sculptor may use many tools apart from woodcarving gouges but the end product is still referred to as wood-carving.

Within the confines of this book the term *wood-carving* will be synonymous with *wood-sculpture* or wood shaping or whatever term may be most applicable. There is no desire to reincarnate the tradition of English woodcarving, only one to encourage the use of wood as a medium to interpret an idea into a tangible three-dimensional object. Towards this end it is emminently suited. There must be few places on this earth where it is not available in some shape or form and at reasonable cost and in most countries a wide variety of species are readily at hand, although size is sometimes a problem. It ranges from the coal-blackness of ebony to the virgin whiteness of holly; the spongy softness of balsa to the glass-hardness of lignum vitae; it can be painted, stained, burnt, sand-blasted, cut, scraped, sanded, drilled, turned, glued; the possibilities are endless. Few, if any, other materials can offer such infinitely varied potential uses as wood. It has been used for monumental statues and minute pieces of jewellery with equal success, and almost anything can and has been achieved with the most unlikely and humble of tools from flint chips to chain-saws.

It is said that the creative urge is present in most people, but it would seem that for most of them the urge is never fulfilled. The reasons for this are obviously very varied, but what is apparent is that few are able to focus their creative urge into a particular channel. Within the minority who elect to carve wood, there is the majority who do not know what to carve. Those who do know can be subdivided again into those who do and don't know *why* they want to carve whatever it is and what they hope to achieve. The best answer to these questions is found by carving itself; get on and carve something, anything, and gradually ideas will crystallize into objectives. However, the serious student of woodcarving should always bear in mind that what he is going to undertake is no mean task, it will take him many hours of concentrated hard work, cost him a significant sum of money, and cause considerable frustration and, at times, despair. Do not take it on lightly, as one might play the odd game of tennis, equip yourself as well as you can, use the best materials you can lay your hands on, leave no stone unturned in order to know your subject, and put into it everything you can. It may be slow and difficult, but you can achieve the highest levels of art if you give enough of yourself. Do not envy the slick virtuosity of the trained professional carver—he trained in a hard school that left him with little time for self-expression and he will probably never regain what you have—the urge to

transform your vision into wood.

Without too much effort you can carve an object—a dog if you like—and show it to your friends and give it to Uncle George for Christmas, and everyone will pat you on the back and say what a damn fine chap you are; tell their friends that you do a bit of woodcarving and made a lovely dog. Then you can be pleased with yourself and Uncle George will stick it on top of the telly and Auntie will dust it every week until someone steps on it or the real dog eats it. But you won't be too upset because since then you've made a cat for Grandma, and a kangaroo for Alf in Australia, and so on. If you can do this you are exceptionally fortunate because there is a silent majority in the background who have never managed to make anything that satisfied themselves or particularly pleased anyone else. It has taken me many years of work to find out what I am trying to achieve and to get the satisfaction and fulfilment of partially achieving it. One tends to aim at the limited objective in most endeavours— the fortunate few who have the foresight to see an overall goal are usually counted amongst the successful people of the world.

Before you take up wood sculpture, before you buy some tools or a block of wood, or pick up a chisel, ask yourself what you are trying to achieve. You may not have a long term answer, but there should be an immediate aim, even if it is only to get relaxation out of using the tools. Whatever the answer, bear it in mind always, and with every move you make on the piece, ask yourself what contribution it is making towards that end. Many artists and sculptors of the past are now being accused of being slavish imitators of nature. Only a very deluded person would expect to successfully imitate a natural object with a piece of wood. All art is an abstraction—a taking from. The function of the artist is to abstract what he requires from the subject and change or add to it as he sees fit. The product of these deliberations constitutes his vision and, interpreted by his technique, becomes the manifestation of his vision that is his work of art.

A persistent problem amongst those attempting to carve objects in the round is "getting behind" the two-dimensional appearance. The fact is that most carvers are going to work from photographs, which is fine, provided they are used in the light of knowledge. The trouble is that they don't take the photographs themselves, but find them in a book or magazine where there is invariably one picture of a particular pose. It is absolutely essential to find out what lies on the hidden sides and how the object appears from different angles. How can you possibly "get behind" the two-dimensional view if you really have no idea of what is behind. Many objects which we consider familiar are relatively unknown to us as a three-dimensional form. Could you, for instance, draw with reasonble accuracy a cross section of your own chest or a horse's neck? The painter does not have these problems but the sculptor has to consider every facet. You must develop a new way of looking at the physical world, seeing not just colour and light, but forms, texture and geometry. Study your own hand as you move the fingers and make a fist—see how the skin folds— tendons appear and disappear—hollows become bumps—a feeling of tension is conveyed as you tighten your grip—the

whole shape changes from a flattish segmented shape to a deeply fissured block. Having observed the infinite variety and subtlety of changing form in one small movement of your hand, how can you conceivably expect to model the simplest natural object merely from a photograph?

Let us suppose that the subject is a shark. Personally, I have never seen a shark in the flesh, but I have seen them on the television, and there are films of them. Try to get hold of one of these films. In the natural history museums there are probably stuffed sharks and shark skeletons. Perhaps somewhere there is a marine park with live sharks and there are certainly plenty of books. Study the movements of other more available live fish—know about your shark so that when you attack the wood you are quite clear about what you are shaping, and why; not just relying on guesswork, carving a vague shape and hoping no-one will notice. The importance of this knowledge of the subject cannot be overemphasised; not only does it give you the confidence in handling your tools that produces good technique, but most significantly, it eliminates that which is not meaningful. For example, through our intimate knowledge of human beings we are well aware that the hands are very expressive and important features— therefore great attention is paid to them and they are looked at very critically. Far less store is placed on the feet. What would be the equivalent features in our shark, or a bird, or a dog? Study the sculpture of the past and present. How did they treat the same feature in ancient Greece and China? What were they trying to say? Did they even see the same things as you see when they looked at a horse or a man? Then look at your subject in the light of accumulated knowledge, and ask yourself "What do I see, and what do I want to say about it?"

A piece of wood sculpture, like any other work of art, is the culmination of a wide ranging number of skills which have been brought together to the greatest ability of the maker and united into a single object. If any one of the necessary skills is lacking or preponderant it will show and the observer will make a judgement accordingly. For example, a high degree of skill in using the tools will be found insufficient if there is distinct lack of sensitivity to texture or imagination. The success of people like Grinling Gibbons was as much due to their flair in design as to their technical expertise. This seems rather obvious, but it seems to be a major stumbling block to so many carvers that this point must be stressed. Every aspect of a carving must be most carefully thought out and considered. The subject itself is the first object of scrutiny. You are probably going to spend many hours of hard work carving it. Is it worthy of your efforts, or is it trivial and unlikely to maintain your interest? Why have you chosen it? What have you got to say about it? Do you have sufficient knowledge to carry it out? Every line of your drawing must be studied—could it be improved by a change here or a removal there? Remember, you are not bound to nature. You, as the artist, must develop sensitivity to line and form, just as you learn to sharpen your tools. Timber must be selected for colour, grain, texture and character, as well as working properties and, where joints are necessary, the posi-

tion of them must be considered and the grain matched. The finish, so often neglected, must be a positive step towards the enhancement of the piece, not an afterthought that you would prefer to forget. To sand a carving totally smooth can take almost as long as the carving, but if it is not done to perfection the finished result can be an appalling, half-finished appearance that completely obscures the merits of the work.

These are just a few of the points that must be thought about. Your audience will judge your work much as you would judge a motor car; every detail must be working correctly, individually and collectively—not some or most, but every one.

To start at the beginning with the choice of subject, a little examination of one's own motives is called for; ask yourself why you want to carve at all. If you have been inspired by carvings you have seen, what was it about them that attracted you? Do you see it as a challenge to achieve a level of technical skill? Are you looking for a suitable medium to express ideas you have? Works of art do not appear in blinding flashes of light; they must be analysed and systematically constructed if you want to achieve a degree of satisfaction and not spend your life saying "it would have been better if I'd done so and so". You must be able to draw your subject, accurately. If you can't draw—learn, or copy or trace or get someone to draw for you, but be sure, that if your drawing is shaky then it is likely that your carving will be so too. And all the time, bear in mind that you are drawing for a carving and what might look fine on paper may be uncarvable, or at least beyond your ability.

2 Wood

THE importance of the wood used for carving cannot be over-emphasised. It can mean the difference between frustration and satisfaction, success and failure. The popular order of priorities seems to be cheapness and ease of procurement — for instance a lump of deal found on the nearest building site. A pile of firewood would be a better hunting ground; here you are likely to find nice little blocks of oak, pear, apple, hawthorn and other hedgerow and garden trees, ideal for carving and quite likely to be reasonably dry. That kind of scavenging is fine for practising and for unimportant bits and pieces but for a serious carving the timber is a major factor in its success.

Carving in the round demands large blocks of wood and 5″-6″ (127mm-152mm) is as big as you are likely to find in a good timber yard, well seasoned and free of cracks. But even 6″×6″ (152mm× 152mm) will not produce a very large piece of work and the restrictions of the straight square shape will be a great source of irritation. This leaves two alternatives: either you find large blocks of wood or you join smaller blocks together. I have found large blocks in different places from time to time. Old beams, as big as 14″ (355mm) square turn up, but are invariably cracked, worm eaten, full of nails or all three. If not, they provide excellent carving material. Sawmills and woodworking establishments that use large quantities of timber are probably the best source. I have obtained excellent limewood 12″ (304mm) square from a monastery that has its own sawmill, and also from a pallet making company that uses literally any kind of timber that comes to hand. Being totally uninterested in the quality of the wood, any piece that is not of use is thrown in a corner and forgotten. The only way to find large blocks of wood is to hunt them down, but having acquired them remember you have a very dubious asset. Even if it is of sufficient age to be completely dry, and is fault free, the tensions that may be released when you cut into it could tear it apart.

Another problem is the amount of wood that needs removing from the block. Apart from the colossal waste that may be involved, the time and effort are likely to be enormous, and considering the other factors, solid blocks do not seem to be a realistic alternative for carvings of any size. By comparison, laminating or joining smaller blocks together seems to be the easy option. However, the problems inherent in laminating are as serious as those of the large blocks. Firstly, the timber must be planed perfectly flat in order to obtain perfect joints. This would appear straight forward enough, but remember that the joints may look fine on the outside, but if there is the slightest hollowing of the surfaces it will appear as a crack when the wood is cut into. In other words disaster can happen half way through the carving after many hours of work. Also the colour and grain of the adjacent block must be an excellent match if you want the joints to be anything less than obvious. Difficulty will be experienced in carving if the grain does not all run the same way, and the adjacent end grains will look like an abstract collage if they are not matched. The next problem is shrinkage. When the carving is complete and the different blocks are reduced to very unequally shaped pieces, they are likely to expand and contract at very different rates and your joints are liable to give way. One of my own carvings has a joint which opens and closes according to the weather. The last and possibly worst problem is the finishing. Different pieces of the same wood will absorb stains and polishes at different rates; for instance the sapwood and heartwood of lime are virtually indistinguishable when freshly cut, but they may change dramatically when a coat of sealer is applied or when stained. Suddenly you are confronted with a two-tone carving, and there is little you can do about it, and if you've been really careless you may have a pretty white line of glue running between them. Of course these are technical problems and can be overcome, but the significant point here is that one must be prepared to expend a considerable amount of time and trouble selecting and preparing the timber.

Usually the wood used for laminating is cut to the maximum required size, glued up and subsequently bandsawn. However, it sometimes happens that this is very wasteful or it is easier to cut the wood first. For example in Fig. 1 the horse's body is to be made in three sections: the hind legs, the trunk and the forelegs. It would be pointless making up a huge block and cutting it up. It is far better to shape the blocks first and then glue them up. Similarly, it can be seen in the Falstaff project, Fig. 217 the right leg, and Fig. 219 the right arm, are bandsawn separately and applied.

Which timber you use is a more difficult and subjective question and one which must be related to the subjects of the carving. Highly figured woods are a two edged sword. They are beautiful and exciting to work, but most exotic figuring is caused by wild and erratic grain structures which can be extremely difficult to

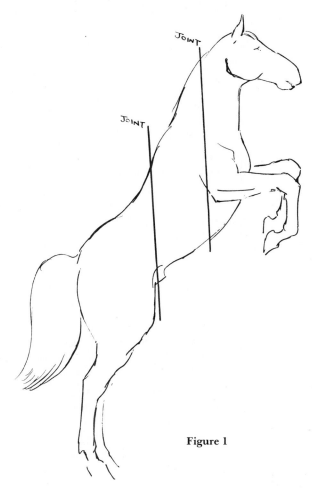

Figure 1

carve. On the other hand the patterns in the wood can make a plain carving more interesting. The pronounced black stripes in the walnut of "Harlequin" are intended as a reminder of his patchwork suit. The silky flames on the Gyr falcon's back make it perhaps more attractive than the detailed front view. As a general rule I would say, avoid highly figured wood and if it is to be used, then the carving must be designed to accommodate it.

As previously stated, wood should be dry and free from knots and cracks, the grain should be suitable to the work in hand and the cutting quality of the wood should be in keeping with the type of cutting required.

Apple See Fruitwoods

Ash
Ash is one timber I find unpleasant and difficult to carve. It is coarse and stringy, but it will depend on the particular piece.

Beech
Probably one of the most versatile and reliable woods in use. It is cheap, freely available, stable, cuts easily and cleanly, will take fine detail, polishes beautifully and is very strong. There is little you can not do with beech and it is the backbone of the furniture industry. Unfortunately it is considered unattractive and is seldom used in its natural state as a show timber. However, odd pieces of beech can be found which have some unusual feature and can be very beautiful.

Birch
If it is mentioned in woodworking books at all, birch is described as a utility wood for making cheap turnery, bedframes etc. Its remarkable carving qualities are never mentioned but a great deal of Scandinavian work of the finest quality was carried out in birch. It is capable of holding the finest detail, cuts cleanly and easily and should be available in large pieces fairly cheaply.

Boxwood, English
This is the ultimate wood for carving minute detail. The grain structure is almost invisible. It is a lovely butter colour, occasionally with dark streaks, and has a sweet smell. It is very hard and dense, cuts cleanly and easily and takes a beautiful polish. Unfortunately it grows only as a small bush, 3″-4″ (76mm-101mm) diameter logs would be average, 6″ (152mm) diameter most unusual. Hence it has to be left in the round and as such it is very difficult to season without splitting. It is expensive to buy but since you will only need a small piece, it is well worth paying for a good seasoned block.

Cedar See Softwoods

Cherry See Fruitwoods

Chestnut
It has been frequently used in the past for carving, in fact, I believe that much of the carved 'oak' one sees in churches is in fact chestnut.

Elm
Elm is not traditionally a carving wood, but has been used extensively in recent

years because of its availability, cheapness and great size whilst being very resistant to splitting. It is fine for very large pieces, but is not suitable for smaller intricate work, being a rather coarse wood.

Fruitwoods

Most of the timbers from fruit trees are pleasant to work and will take very fine detail. They are, however, difficult to obtain in usable sizes being exceptionally prone to splitting, especially if left in the log, and since the trees are generally small, that is the only way to get decent sized pieces. **Cherry** can usually be acquired from good timber merchants, as can **pear** which is considered to be the best for carving. Personally, I prefer **plum**, which is very fine grained and beautifully coloured. **Apple** is perhaps the commonest, although, fortunately for carvers, there seems always to be more pear around, probably due to its shorter life and larger dimensions which are kept rather than discarded. It carves well and has a fine grain and texture with darker zones than pear, and is harder. It is used more in turnery, and saw handles and cogs were often made from it. Most fruit trees end up as firewood so you should be able to acquire the green logs for virtually nothing, and a rummage through an old log pile may be well rewarded.

Hawthorn

A hedgerow tree which may reach diameters of 15″ (380mm) or so, it is almost invariably cut up and burnt. I have never seen a dry piece for sale, but it is a white hard wood of very fine texture and although I have never used it personally I am told on good authority that it is the equal of boxwood for carving very fine detail. Its greater dimensions and availability would certainly recommend it.

Holly

A very fine, hard wood, excellent for carving and capable of the finest detail and a beautiful finish. American holly is claimed to be better, whiter and available in larger sizes.

Jelutong

Also recommended for carving in America. I, personally, have found it appalling. It is very soft, characterless and thoroughly dissatisfying.

Laburnum

Hard, and solid, this beautiful wood can be successfully carved but is not easily found in sizes useful for a carver.

Lignum Vitae

Full marks to anyone who takes a gouge to a piece of lignum vitae. It is almost glass hard and wearing goggles would be recommended. By using rotary burrs, files and grinders, no doubt a very pleasing result could be obtained, but I suspect that the oily nature of the wood would clog them rapidly.

Lime

Definitely the woodcarver's wood: a beautiful creamy colour with occasional brown patches and streaks, it cuts perfectly and easily in any direction. Some of the finest carving in the world was done in lime, not just by Grinling Gibbons in England but in most European countries, particularly southern Germany. Its fine grain and clean, easy cutting facilitates the most delicate work, whilst the great size of the trees produce timber of large dimension and fairly low price. Using lime comes as a revelation to carvers who have not experienced the pleasure of cutting it. It has an attractive 'pure' quality when polished and after many years its colour deepens to a golden brown.

Mahogany

Quite freely available kiln dried and in large dimensions, a board 24″ (609mm) wide and 4″ or 5″ (101mm-127mm) thick is not unusual. There are so many woods now referred to as mahogany that it is difficult to say which one you may have bought. It is very variable in its working quality and is invariably cursed with interlocked grain, which effectively means that the grain runs in opposite directions in adjacent narrow bands, and this can be very tiresome. The mahogany used now is a light pinkish wood totally unlike the dark brown, hard, heavy Cuban mahogany which was originally employed for furniture. This is virtually unobtainable other than from old furniture and is much sought after by furniture restorers. Honduras (Spanish) mahogany is still available and is the best to use. Very sharp tools are needed and these are blunted fairly quickly by the chalky deposit in the pores. It is ideal for large and medium sized pieces, but tends to be somewhat fragile across the grain when used on very fine detail. It stains and polishes very well and can have beautiful figuring on larger pieces.

Maple

Very hard, creamy coloured wood, which can be successfully used for fine work, but seldom is.

Oak

The backbone of English woodcarving, strong and masculine, it is capable of almost any kind of work, although not well suited to fine, elegant, detailed pieces. Common in churches and houses throughout Europe, its use for carving started in mediaeval Germany and spread across the continent to Britain. Good quality English oak is now becoming somewhat difficult to obtain, especially quarter sawn, which is more stable and shows ray figuring. At its best, straight grained, fast grown oak is fairly soft, easy to work and beautiful to look at. At its worst, it is hard, twisting in the grain, knotty and intractable. Reclaimed oak, such as gate posts or beams, provide large pieces; the wood has usually darkened to a beautiful warm brown and although hard, cuts very cleanly and is aesthetically satisfying to work. Japanese oak tends to be straight grained and rather characterless in comparison to English, and of a fairer texture, but not as nice to carve. American oak is best avoided being stringy and coarse; it was much used on cheap oak furniture earlier this century. Oak can be stained and polished by a multitude of methods, but is never better than when left natural and waxed.

Olive wood

Excellent to carve for detailed work. It is hard, fine grained and with fascinating dark streaks in its creamy white body and mellows to a gold brown. Olive is much used in the Mediterranean area for carving and turning.

Padauk

Good to carve, hard, heavy and brilliant orange red when freshly cut. Although it tends to crumble on the thin cross grain edges, I have found it a very satisfying wood for small detailed figures 10″-12″ (254mm-305mm) high. It takes a beautiful polished cut from the chisel and darkens to a deep red.

Pear See Fruitwoods

Pine See Softwoods

Plane

Known as lacewood, it can be carved very well although not traditionally used. The speckled appearance for which it is known is best suited to large plain surfaces rather than more complex shapes.

Plum See Fruitwoods

Poplar

Somewhat similar to lime in appearance and working qualities, and probably used in the past as a substitute for cheaper work.

Rosewood

There are several kinds of rosewood which are not the same type of tree, but the timber has qualities in common. I have not used them all but certainly Indian rosewood is very nice to work. Sharp tools will leave clean polished cuts although thin edges across the grain do tend to crumble. The colour can be almost black to purple, red and orange with black streaks. It is a very beautiful wood, rather expensive, but available in fairly large sections. Madagascar rosewood is not as good to use, being more splintery and less clean-cutting. In both cases the white sapwood is best avoided.

Softwoods

Throughout history various species of softwood have been used for carving with great success, covering work of all types, from the most delicate detail to enormous ship's figure heads. These can be seen in museums described as red pine, cedar, yellow pine, pine, pitch pine, red deal and so on. Positive identification of the many species is difficult, in particular for the average timber-yard who may be turning over whatever is being sent in from homegrown and foreign suppliers. Consequently, the carver is left with a predicament if he requires a specific species to carve, and it may be further aggravated by the fact that many softwoods are unsuitable for carving.

The options open to the carver are few: he can study softwood identification with the aids of appropriate books, magnifier and lens key to whatever grade he feels would be useful for his requirements; he can take a chance when buying pine or other softwoods that it will carve well; or he can, whenever possible, use one of the many excellent hardwoods instead.

Sycamore

A fine grained, fairly soft, creamy coloured wood. It is good to carve, but tends to get very dirty so must be handled carefully immediately before polishing. The rippled sycamore, so attractive in appearance, can be difficult to carve, and the silky effect tends to be lost on shaped surfaces.

Teak

Good for large pieces and easy to carve. It is available in large sizes and is pleasant to work although some people's skins react to it and the dust is irritating. Some difficulty may be experienced gluing it, but modern adhesives will overcome this problem.

Tulip Tree

This is known in America as basswood and is a favoured carving wood. In Britain it is used more by turners than carvers and is similar in texture to limewood.

Walnut

English walnut is excellent for carving and its great variety of grain and figure recommends it for both large and small pieces. The white sapwood is much softer and is best avoided. It is not very strong on short grain and pieces can easily be broken off.

American black walnut is very easy to carve although not considered to be as pleasing to the eye as English.

In the past Italian walnut, harder, finer and paler in colour was considered far superior to the English variety for carving.

Walnut, African

A golden brown wood with pronounced silky bands running down the length caused by interlocked grain. This is far less troublesome than mahogany and the wood carves very easily and quickly. It is soft and splits easily but is fairly cheap and available in large dimensions.

Yew

A beautiful and much sought after wood today. It has virtually been ignored for the traditional furniture trade and rightly so, since, because of its inherent faults it is incredibly wasteful. One would be very fortunate to find a good block without cracks, dead knots or seams of bark in it. Even good boards for building up to a block are hard to find and expensive. However, having acquired a piece it is superb wood to work, cutting cleanly and taking a very high polish. It is very fine and hard and will take the smallest detail although this may become somewhat confused by the strongly marked grain. The striking colours of yew do mellow very quickly to a warm reddish brown and this should be borne in mind when planning a piece of work.

There are many, many others, home-grown and foreign, which may or may not be good to carve; try them out, but bear in mind that you may spend a considerable sum of money on a large block of untried timber that turns out to be totally unsuitable for your purposes. An example of this, was some East Indian ebony, used to make a figure about 12″ (305mm) high. It was almost uncarvable and virtually had to be filed to shape. Subsequently it split badly although very dry, and the piece was a total loss.

3 Equipment

The bench

IT will be difficult to carve without a bench unless the piece is large enough to be free standing. Its size and shape will be dictated by the work to be performed on it. A very strong kitchen table or a heavy cupboard could be used, indeed all manner of items could be found to serve. The basic essentials are weight, strength, rigidity and solidity to avoid any rebound. Also, various implements will be screwed, bolted and clamped to the top. The bench I use for most carving is illustrated in Fig. 2.

The top should be about chest height and approximately 18″ (456mm) square. It is made from two layers of 1½″ (39mm) hardwood with the grain in opposite directions and both screwed very securely to the subframe. The frame is made from 4″×4″ (101mm×101mm) ash with 8″×1½″ (203mm×39mm) rails top and bottom. The whole is put together with ½″ (13mm) coach bolts. It has a floor which supports four 56lb (25.4kg) weights. On the worktop are provisions for a carver's screw, a holdfast and a hydraulic clamp. On the side is a bracket for a large blacksmiths' leg-vice.

This bench is very strong, very heavy and versatile. Made from reclaimed timber such as floor joists or fence posts, the vice and weights easily obtained from scrapyards, it could be made for a few pounds-worth of bolts and a days' work. It requires very little space and one can move around it. Various attachments

Figure 2

such as flexi-shaft and power unit, grinder and shelves for tools and oilstones can easily be fitted, creating a free-standing, independent unit.

Having acquired a bench, the next vital equipment is holding devices.

Vices

Vices come in many shapes and sizes. To hold even a small carving, say 12″ (305mm) high, a vice must exert a very powerful grip to withstand the blows of a mallet. A standard woodworking vice is shown in Fig. 3 and must be large, very strongly tightened and the piece of wood have flat parallel sides to succeed. An engineer's vice, Fig. 4 having a smaller jaw area, exerts a far greater, more concentrated force and will hold more irregular shaped pieces. In doing so, of course, it tends to damage the wood. A partial solution to these problems is to attach the carving blank to another piece of wood which is held in the vice and this is frequently successful. A leg-vice is an old-fashioned blacksmith's vice, similar to the engineer's vice but usually with deeper jaws and enormous leverage. A great deal of carving can be done using only a vice, and it is invaluable to the carver. Good vices are expensive, but secondhand ones can usually be found.

Figure 3

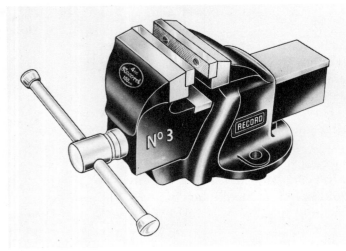

Figure 4

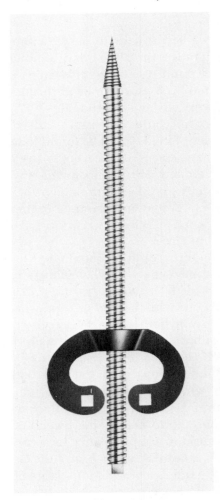

Figure 5

The carver's screw

This is shown in Figs. 5 and 6 and is used for holding blocks to be carved. It is an excellent device, proved throughout history, and being relatively cheap, is unbeatable value for money.

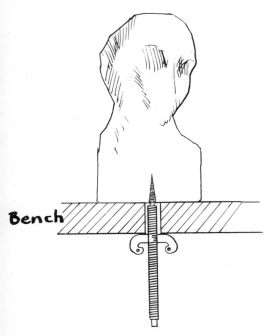

Bench

Figure 6

The holdfast

The holdfast Fig. 7 has limited use, mainly for holding flat boards to the bench top. I find that two are necessary for a really positive grip. Also it requires a very strong bench top to resist the leverage as it is screwed down.

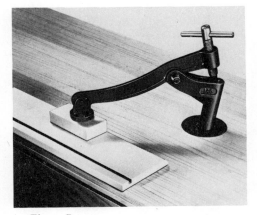

Figure 7

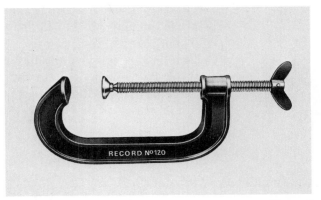

RECORD Nº120

Figure 8

G-Cramps

Fig 8 can be used to hold boards to the bench top for relief carving, lettering, etc. Their use in carving in the round is very limited.

There are various other devices and jigs for holding work. The one I use for most three-dimensional carving is a hydraulically powered universally jointed arm with a faceplate to which the work is attached. There are various sizes which resist different pressures. This machine facilitates carving which would be very difficult or impossible without it, and makes the normal run of work far easier and faster. They are expensive but worth the outlay for the more ambitious carver. One can be seen mounted on the bench-top in Fig. 2.

Carving tools

Carving tools can be roughly divided into those with a cutting edge and those without. Those with a cutting edge include chisels, gouges, knives, axes, adzes, and other pieces of metal that might be sharpened to cut the fibres. Non-edged tools, I would classify as files, rasps, scrapers, drills, burrs, saws, sanders and other grinding and abrasive devices.

Carving chisels and gouges are made in a bewildering variety of shapes and sizes and whilst one can successfully carve with very few it would be a mistake to think that many of these shapes are obsolete or that having plenty of tools is not an advantage. See Fig. 9 and 10.

Handles

The handle is an important feature of a gouge. It has to withstand a tremendous hammering from the mallet and if not properly made will let you down remarkably quickly, especially on larger tools. The best are made from boxwood, but very few carving tools, if any, are fitted with them today. Rosewood is also durable but, likewise, seldom used. Ash is used by some manufacturers, and if well selected it will stand a lot of punishment.

Beech was used a great deal in the past and is still common to-day, although, perhaps because of the quality of the wood, it seems to split and fray quite quickly. Various other woods are used such as bubinga and types of mahogany with varying degrees of success, and some plastic of course. Most handles have a brass ferrule around the neck where the tang enters the wood, to prevent splitting. The ash-handled Swiss chisels that I use do not have a ferrule and seem none the worse.

Handles are made in a variety of shapes and there is no particular superiority in any one, other than the fact that hexagonal ones do not tend to roll about so easily; a tool rolling off the bench can be severely damaged on a stone floor. Although a range of tools all with matching handles may look very smart and

Figure 9

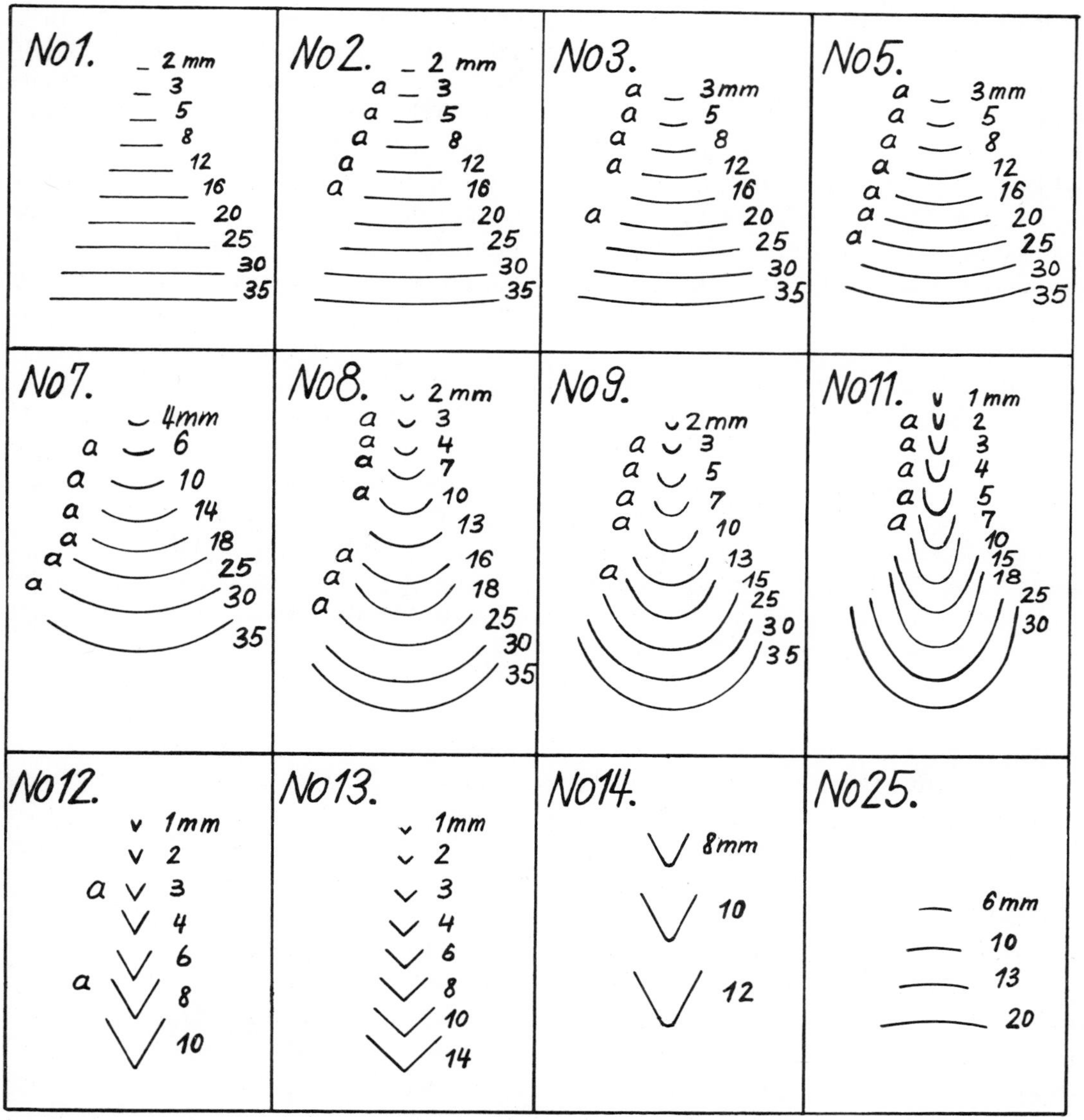

No1.	No2.	No3.	No5.
2 mm	a 2 mm	a 3mm	a 3mm
3	a 3	a 5	a 5
5	a 5	a 8	a 8
8	a 8	a 12	a 12
12	a 12	16	a 16
16	a 16	a 20	a 20
20	20	25	a 25
25	25	30	30
30	30	35	35
35	35		

No7.	No8.	No9.	No11.
4mm	a 2 mm	2mm	a 1mm
a 6	a 3	a 3	a 2
a 10	a 4	a 5	a 3
a 14	a 7	a 7	a 4
a 18	a 10	a 10	a 5
a 25	13	13	a 7
a 30	a 16	15	10
35	a 18	25	15
	a 25	30	18
	30	35	25
	35		30

No12.	No13.	No14.	No25.
v 1mm	v 1mm	V 8mm	6mm
v 2	v 2	10	10
a v 3	v 3	12	13
v 4	v 4		20
v 6	v 6		
a v 8	v 8		
v 10	v 10		
	v 14		

Figure 10

pleasing, it is in fact an advantage to have a range of distinguishing marks about them. It can take literally minutes at a time to find a particular size of gouge amongst forty or fifty of exactly the same appearance.

Carving chisels can be bought unhandled, although the cost of making your own is usually uneconomical. If you do, make sure your handles are comfortable and long enough or your hand and your work will suffer. Make sure also, that the blade and handle are exactly in alignment otherwise your mallet blows will not be transmitted directly to the cutting edge. Be sure to fit the tang tightly into the handle, but be careful not to split it as it is driven on.

Blades

Many craftsmen today are obsessed with old tools. One has only to look at pre-war tools and machinery to see why this reaction has taken the path it has. Well designed and constructed, from the largest cast planer to the smallest pair of callipers, there is often a sense of rightness about them that is at one with a fine piece of timber and a dedicated craftsman. It would be unfair and untrue to say that there are no good tools made today or that modern technology has not made brilliant innovations, but they must be carefully sought out and often worked on to get them into good working condition. Good tools are expensive and important to you. They should be cared for and maintained in perfect working order; a good chisel or gouge should be razor sharp, clean and polished. Several companies still make carving tools in Britain, in a range of 2,000—3,000 shapes but their quality is variable. Like so many products to-day they seem to be happier to replace faulty products than enforce quality control. Hence there is no standard set and the tool you buy may be good, bad or indifferent purely by chance. Personally, I use old pre-war gouges made by Herring and Addis and the new ones of Swiss manufacture which are beautifully made and of uniformly excellent steel. The old British ones are always good, though whether this was because of the steel as most people say, or because only the good ones have survived is debatable.

There seem to have been innumerable manufacturers of chisels in bygone days. How reputable they were I have no idea. Apparently the tools were made of high carbon steel which was hardened, tempered and ground by hand. It follows therefore that there would have been differences in the quality of steel and the skill of the craftsman. Certainly, some of them seem to be hardened for the first couple of inches only. However, they are invariably well shaped and hold a good edge. They can still be bought in second-hand shops and auctions although prices can be little, if any, cheaper than new ones.

New tools should be made of high quality carbon steel which has been hardened, tempered and ground. The metal should harden to a specific level on the Rockwell scale and although you cannot check this without expert help, experience will show you when a tool does not hold a good edge. The flute down the blade of a V tool should be well shaped, dead straight and even, and the thickness of the edges identical. Look through all the chisels in stock until you find one that completely satisfies you.

The point I am making here is that acquiring good carving tools is not a cut and dried business. Generally speaking, the tools will be ground to a bevel which may or may not be correct and not until you have sharpened it correctly can you tell if the tool is a good one. The Swiss tools I use are razor sharp when bought and I feel this is a great advantage to the beginner since it gives him a model of what the cutting edge should be like. To achieve this cutting edge is an art in itself.

The mallet

I am frequently asked why woodcarving mallets (Fig. 11) are basically spherical

Figure 11

rather than flat-faced like carpenters' mallets. One may as well ask why carpenters' mallets are flat. I believe the carver's shape is far older than the carpenter's and with good reason. If a flat-faced mallet is not reasonably square to the chisel handle it will glance off, but with a carver's mallet this is not necessary. Also a far smaller area of the round mallet hits the handle and I think this causes less damage. Mallets should be made of lignum vitae for weight and hardness. Using lighter woods such as beech would mean that the mallet would have to be either very large or very light. Also it will soon start to flake and split. Light mallets lack control becuse they must be swung harder. The lignum vitae should be the dark heartwood, not the yellow sapwood as this is also lighter and prone to flaking. The handle is less important—ash, beech or a similar strong timber will do.

The bandsaw

This is not an essential tool to the carver. I would say it occupies the same position as the circular saw to a cabinet maker; you can live without it but at the expense of a lot of hard work, and the cabinet maker after all, does buy his timber cut roughly to size. The bandsaw can be replaced to some extent by the bow saw but its use is limited. A good bandsaw with a depth of cut of 6″(152mm) or more enables you to remove large amounts of waste in a few minutes instead of hours and days with a gouge. More important, it makes possible the accurate cutting of the

Figure 12
A. Surform
B. Rasp
C. Halfround
   file
D. Round file
E. Warding file
F. Diamond file
G. Riffler file
H.   ,,   ,,
I.   ,,   ,,
J. Diamond file

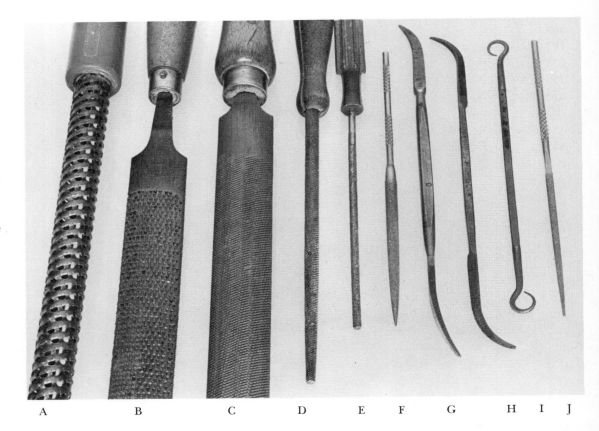

A   B   C   D   E   F   G   H   I   J

profile of a carving, from one, two or three directions. This gives you an immeasurable advantage over someone starting straight into the block with a gouge. This will become apparent in the projects. Obviously a bandsaw is a large investment of money which many will not be prepared to make, but it should not be difficult to find a local joiner or timber yard that will saw your carvings for a very moderate payment.

Files and rasps
Rasps are coarse files for use on wood. Although I seldom use them myself, they are very efficient tools for shaping larger carvings. Files are finer and come in many shapes, sizes and grades. They are very useful for removing tool cuts prior to sanding and for actual shaping of certain parts. All the different sizes of files are worth having, from large, coarse bastards down to delicate, fine needle files. Rifflers are very small shaped files which may be invaluable for cleaning up hollows and corners. The ones to buy are diemakers' rifflers for use on metal. Those sold for woodcarving which have the hooked teeth of a rasp are pretty useless. Another excellent type available is diamond files. These are needle files with diamond dust embedded in nickel plate on the surface. The great advantage of them is that unlike an ordinary file, they cut in any direction and leave what looks like a sanded surface. See figure 12.

Punches

In the past, punches were used extensively for texturing the surface; indeed, one German limewood relief carving shows evidence of the use of twenty-six different types. Forty or fifty patterns are available today but I think they are seldom used. At times they can be used to good effect but I usually make my own from silver steel. Fig. 13

Rotary Burrs

There are many types and qualities of burr and a selection is shown in Fig. 14. These small multi-fluted cutters on shanks, range from minute dental drills to fairly large rasp-like affairs. There are diamond burrs, tungsten burrs, tiny grindstones, sanders and cutting discs. They are normally used in a flexibly-shafted hand-set (Fig. 15) running at anything between 3,000 and 30,000 revolutions per minute. I have one and use it for certain purposes, undercutting and fragile details, where it may do what

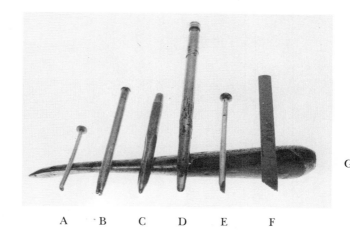

Figure 13. Punches
A. Ring shaped punch, bent at right angle. Made from a nail.
B. 3-Ring punch made from steel rod.
C and D. Round nose punches for ukibori.
E. Straight-edged punch made from a nail.
F. Factory made matting punch for backgrounds of relief carvings.
G. Ukibori punch, for raising line, pressure applied by the hand. Made from a screwdriver.

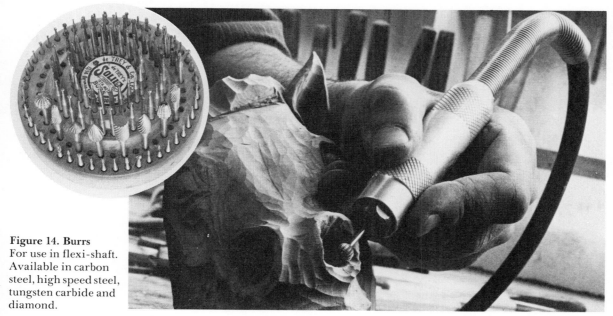

Figure 14. Burrs
For use in flexi-shaft. Available in carbon steel, high speed steel, tungsten carbide and diamond.

Figure 15

would be nearly impossible with a chisel. Some people use nothing else.

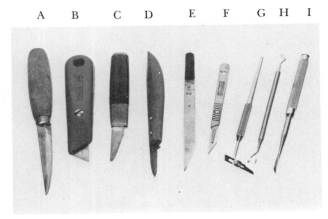

Figure 16

A. Swedish sloyd knife. Laminated steel blade.
B. Stanley knife.
C. American chip carving knife.
D. German chip carving knife.
E. Japanese laminated steel knife.
F. Surgical scalpel.
G. Dental surgical knife, replaceable scalpel blade.
H. Dental scraper.
I. Dental bone chisel.

Knives

These are used far more in America than in Britain, where a wide variety of shapes and types are available and extremely complex detailed work is performed. Many of the styles can be ground to shape from ordinary knives and pieces of tool steel. The techniques of using whittling knives is radically different to that of gouges. The work is usually hand held and the knife cut is towards the user against the pressure of thumb. Although a clear division is drawn between carving and whittling, I see no reason why the two techniques cannot be used to compliment each other. Fig. 16

Measuring instruments

Apart from the standard tape measures and rulers I would recommend the acquisition of a couple of pairs of callipers, one large and one small and perhaps a vernier gauge since it has the measurements written on it. A very useful gadget is a pair of ratio callipers, this has points at both ends with a sliding pivot which can be moved to give different ratios between the two sets of points. It is invaluable for taking direct measurements from a photo or drawing onto the carving. Fig. 17

There are many other tools used from time to time. Planes for preparing timber for gluing, saws, drills, sanders, etc. Those which you do not have you must borrow or eventually buy.

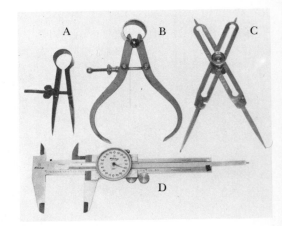

Figure 17

A. A pair of spring dividers.
B. Outside callipers.
C. Ratio callipers, adjustable from 1:1 to 1:10.
D. Vernier gauge.

4 Sharpening

Sharpening

I feel it is wrong to set down a formula for sharpening a carving tool. With a flat chisel or a plane iron, given a perfectly flat oil stone, if the correct angle is maintained and the steel is moved to and fro with even pressure, then a perfect bevel should result and hence a perfect cutting edge. With the vast range of curves in carving tools it is extremely difficult to achieve this perfection. It is necessary, firstly, to understand the basic principles of sharpening.

Sharpening stones are graded in grit sizes, the finer the grit, the smoother the stone, the sharper the edge produced. The particles of grit wear away the metal and produce a thin wire of steel at the edge. When the filament of steel joining this wire edge to the bevel breaks, the broken edge left on the chisel is the cutting edge. The finer the grit of the stone, the thinner this filament is when it breaks and the sharper is the cutting edge. It is broken off by bending it back and forth using the oil stone on the outside and the slip stone on the inside. It should be clear, therefore, that to accomplish this with precision on, say ⅛" (3mm) U-shaped gouge is not easy.

The finest grit sharpening stones easily available are Japanese water stones which run to 6000 grit. This leaves a mirror finish on steel. Unfortunately they are so soft that the thin edge of the gouge rapidly ploughs into the surface. The next finest stone is the Hard Black

Arkansas. This is a natural stone, quarried in America from a spar of noviculite which is almost pure quartz. It is extremely hard, virtually unmarkable with tool steel, and considering its fineness, very fast cutting. It is expensive, but you do not need a full-sized bench stone, and it will give you a perfect edge for many years and well-worth the investment. Other stones available, are, in my opinion, not worth bothering with, apart from a slightly coarser stone for removing large amounts of metal in the event of chipping a gouge. The final finish is given to the gouge by stropping it on a piece of leather dressed with a fine abrasive powder, which in fact substitutes the very fine Japanese 6000 grit mentioned above. Figs. 18 and 19 show a selection of bench and slipstones and strops.

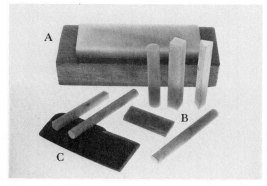

Figure 18. Oilstones
A. White Arkansas bench stone.
B. A selection of arkansas slip stone.
C. Multipurpose slip-stone, home made from slate.

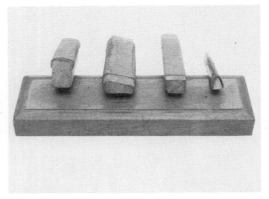

Figure 19. Strops
Made from leather glued to shaped pieces of wood and dressed with crocus powder.

In principle, the gouge is held in both hands, the bevel laid on the oil stone and the tool moved around the surface while rotating it around the curve of the bevel. Figs. 20, 21 and 22. This should wear away the steel evenly and produce a wire edge all around the curve. However, what invariably happens in unskilled hands is that the corners of the gouge tend to get caught on the stone which rounds them off, or a particular part of the curve wears more than the rest and a wavy cutting edge results. In deep gouges this is usually seen as deep bites out of the bottom of the curve, and on shallow gouges, the corners severely worn back, leaving a curved cutting edge. On very small gouges the effects can be disastrous. Although the method described above must be used, the effects on the edge must be carefully and minutely monitored. Any tool grinder, using highly sophisticated machinery will inspect the effects regularly with a jeweller's eyepiece. Any tendency to deviate from the straight square edge must immediately be countered by lesser or greater pressure as appropriate. Smaller gouges might well be held up to the light and the oilstone taken to the tool. Beware of the wire edge deceiving you, for it can appear to be the solid metal, suddenly breaking off to reveal a drastic error.

Equally dangerous are slipstones. They never fit the gouge shape properly and, if used carelessly, oversized ones will take off the corners and undersized ones make deep scoops in the curved edge.

Figure 20

Figure 21

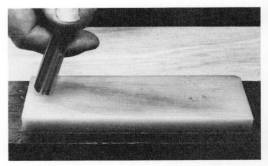

Figure 22

The V tool is often treated as if it were two flat chisels joined edge to edge, and sharpened as such. This produces a hook protruding at the point of the V. The triangular slipstone aggravates this by taking out two scoops just above the hook. The result is useless. The V tool must be treated as a minutely small gouge with its two sides extended into long flat surfaces. By all means hone the flats like chisels but roll the V like a gouge. Use the slipstone carefully, tickling the edge with it, not just sliding it up and down. Basically, you simply have to fiddle around with the edge until you get it right. Fig. 23 and 24.

The question of the length or angle of the bevel are a subject of dispute. Some authorities maintain that short bevels should be used for heavy work and harder wood, since long thin edges would easily break. Others solve this same problem by putting another small bevel on the inside of the gouge, thus increasing the angle of the bevel. Some say do this only on a large gouge for roughing out, and have long thin bevels for delicate work. Opinion also varies about the heel of the bevel, one view being that it should be left sharp as on a carpenter's chisel, another that the whole bevel should be curved. It has been suggested that the function of the inside bevel is to centralise the cutting edge in the thickness of the steel for the purposes of accuracy, also, that without it the tool tends to bury itself in the wood rather than scooping out the cut. The variations of opinion about carving tool bevels seem endless.

My own view is that different carvers use different woods for different purposes and shape their tools to suit. The Swiss carver, using mainly soft limewood or pine uses long thin bevels to make thin delicate cuts. The English carver working in oak making deep heavy cuts for church pews and so on needs a stronger bevel on a heavier tool. Personally I use a long bevel without an inside one. True, on some types of wood they blunt quickly, but I cannot regrind my tools for different pieces of work.

The important part about sharpening is this, without sharp tools you will not produce satisfactory work, and it will show. Carving tools must be sharpened

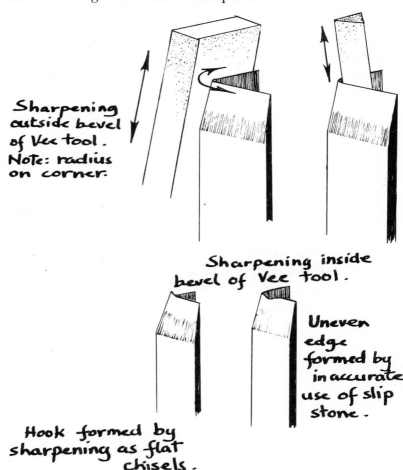

Sharpening outside bevel of Vee tool. Note: radius on corner.

Sharpening inside bevel of Vee tool.

Uneven edge formed by inaccurate use of slip stone.

Hook formed by sharpening as flat chisels.

Figure 23

A   B   C   D   E

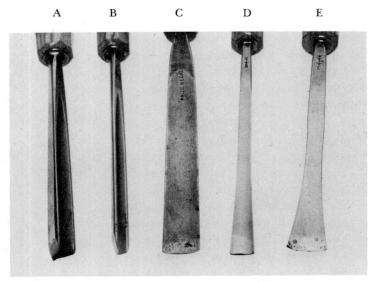

Figure 24. Chisels
A. Badly sharpened V tool—note the wavy edge and hook.
B. Correctly sharpened V tool.
C. Badly sharpened gouge—note curved edge and rounded corner.
D. Correctly sharpened gouge.
E. Damaged edge caused by cutting African Blackwood.

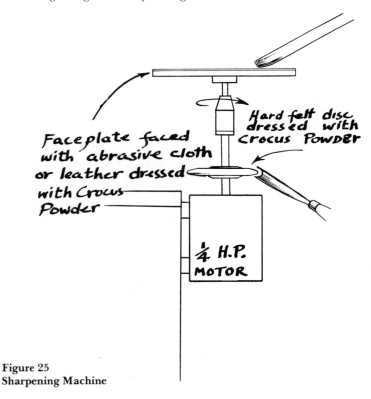

Figure 25
Sharpening Machine

constantly, not every week or every day, but every few minutes while they are in use. This sounds an onerous task. We are all inclined to be lazy and avoid irritating repetitive tasks. The answer therefore is to make sharpening easy.

I sharpen all my tools on a machine which does the work of two minutes in five seconds. The device illustrated on the side of the bench Fig. 2 and Fig. 25 consists of a ¼ H.P. motor fitted with a chuck incorporating a pair of flanges for a grind stone. These are readily available to fit various sizes of shaft. Three faceplates are made using plywood and arbors. To one is glued 120 grit abrasive cloth, to the second 180 grit and to the third, leather, dressed with crocus powder.

The gouge is held on to the rotating disc in the same manner as an oil stone. By moving from the outer edge towards the centre, the surface running speed is reduced to almost zero, thus total control is established. The 120 grit is only to remove large amounts of metal. The 180 grit replaces the oilstone and the leather represents a high speed strop which, if used frequently will keep a gouge sharp for many hours of use. The inside of the gouge is stropped in a shaped leather or hard felt disc also treated with crocus powder, fixed between the flanges. This device is bolted to the side of the bench, with a handy switch. Keeping tools sharp thus becomes a minor consideration, and for less than the price of an oil stone. There are machines on the market which will produce extremely sharp edges on tools. Prices vary, the actual method employed is basically the same but to my knowledge none of them have the facility for the inside of gouges.

5 Polishing and Mounting

THE finish on a carving may not be quite as important as it is on a piece of furniture, but the same principles still apply. There is no easy way to achieve a good finish—the work must be done either in the preparation or in the polishing. Obviously it is the work of seconds to put teak oil on a piece. but it will show every minute blemish in the surface. French polishing, on the other hand, may be difficult and time consuming but it does have certain filling and 'glossing over' abilities. Wax polishing, I feel, needs time to achieve a good patina.

There are so many ways of finishing a piece of wood that entire books have been written on the subject and even they only give one man's way of doing it. I can only list those I have used myself and I would refer the reader to more specialized works to find out more.

As I have said before, the groundwork is most important; sanding a carving to perfection can take days, sometimes longer than the carving. A good tooled finish can take almost as long.

Wax Polishing

After careful sanding to the finest grit or tooling, the wood needs to be sealed. I use brown or white shellac sealer although diluted polyurethane would presumably work, but shellac sands down very easily; when dry, rub down with flour paper or fine steel wool. Dust off meticulously and wax. Wax polish comes in a wide range of formulae and qualities, containing more or less of this or that wax dissolved in this or that liquid. Also, you can make your own with beeswax and turpentine, but I have always found it hard work to use. What I think is important is that some wax polishes dry in seconds and must be rubbed immediately. This is fine on a table top, but on carvings, deposits of wax in corners and fine details will go very hard and turn white and you can end up spending hours with a knife picking it out again, or washing the whole carving in turpentine.

I think wax polish is best applied with a tooth brush or an artist's bristle brush, taking care not to leave deposits in corners, and then carefully polished with a similar clean brush, and finally buffed with a clean duster. This should result in a pleasant sheen, which will probably disappear over a short period, a week or two. The process really needs repeating three or four times over in the following week or two and an occasional waxing every few weeks. Little and often is infinitely better than a massive dose. In a years' time when the wood has mellowed slightly and a burnished shine has been created, your carving should look 100% better than the day you finished it. If on the other hand it is never waxed again, as so often happens, it will become dull, dry and possibly cracked.

Polyurethane

Modern synthetic resins and traditional varnishes are regarded as the wrong thing to use on carvings. However, if a piece of sculpture is to go outside they are really the best way of protecting the wood. If polyurethane is applied thinly in diluted coats and rubbed down between coats, it can give an excellent finish which is extremely durable. It does not have to look like treacle.

Oil

Danish oil, teak oil, tung oil and other proprietary finishing oils are applied directly to the wood and certainly enhance the colour and grain. Also, they have the advantage of allowing you to recarve or sand after oiling without showing the slightest mark when the oil is re-applied. This is not so with many other finishes. However you will get only the dullest of shines on the wood and dust tends to stick in the corners.

Linseed oil is somewhat different. I make a mixture of equal parts boiled linseed oil and turpentine and heat it to around boiling point in a double-boiler. I then brush this on to the wood freely, leave it for a couple of hours to soak in and then wipe off very thoroughly. This is then left to dry for about a week, depending on the atmosphere. When the surface is completely dry, rub down with fine steel wool. This will leave a silky smooth, shiny surface. The lightest coating of wax will now produce a good permanent shine, with a far richer and deeper colour than wax alone would. Also the wood is water proof.

French polish

This process is difficult enough on flat surfaces. On carvings, I think it is best applied with the special brushes which are available, in very thin, diluted coats.

Of course an expert french polisher will produce a beautiful finish by methods he will keep to himself. It can look good if done well, but you can ruin a carving with french polish if you are not careful.

Paint

I have painted very few carvings. In order to make a limewood horse black I stained it black, then gave it three or four coats of matt black black-board paint, rubbing down with flour paper after each coat, and finally polishing with black wax polish. The result was excellent, rather like a black bronze.

I think the main difficulty is that the pores of the wood show through the paint, so a great deal of rubbing down is required. However, painted woodcarvings were once the norm rather than the exception and it is still done quite often.

Of course what finish you use is dictated to a certain extent by the nature of the carving. Very delicate detail may not take kindly to the rubbing necessary for waxing, and some carvings look very well left completely unpolished.

The finishing touch to a carving is the display stand, plinth or mount. This is a very subjective decision that you must make, which can have a significant affect on the impact of the sculpture. There are several considerations which may or may not influence your decision. If you know the final resting place of the piece, this must be taken into account, also the wishes of the customer may be a factor, and cost and availability of materials cannot be ignored. Of course the carving often creates its own base such as the Toad figure in the projects section; or may not need one, such as the Still Life.

I think the real difference lies in the audience reaction to a sculpture. The Horse, when stood on a sideboard, on its own legs is appreciated as an ornament; stood on a polished block of wood it is regarded more as a piece of serious sculpture; mounted on a slab of marble with an engraved brass plate, it is taken as a portrait of a particular racehorse, of more socio-historical importance than artistic. The Caterpillar, on the other hand, would look rather ridiculous mounted on an ostentatious marble plinth.

I feel there should be a contrast between carving and plinth, whether of material, colour or texture. The rich brown oak head of the Pony is placed on a smoothly polished block of white oak. It is a functional base for a straight portrait of the animal, the name to be added later. The contrast is confined to the colour of the wood and the flatness of the surfaces. The Stingray goes further, having a base of green and white marble, reminiscent of foaming sea water, providing a contrast in shape, colour and material; texture is still basically the same. The Gyr falcon however, goes all the way, being mounted on a block of grey and white unpolished marble—a contrast of material, colour, texture and shape.

Size presents another decision to be made. In an art gallery you will see tiny sculptures on huge plinths, and larger than life figures with their feet on the floor. Harlequin stands on a block of figured sycamore about 8″ (202mm) high. His feet project over the edges, back and front; in other words he is on a square column, too small for him to stand on and disproportionately tall. I felt this would accentuate the feeling that he was running along and "lighten" the whole figure. The Black Bull has virtually no base, just a ½″ (12mm) of blackwood under his feet. Apart from the fact that the uniformity of the series he is part of demands that it be so, I think it helps convey the impression of a large powerful animal, dwarfing the base he is sat on. The Torso figure could be left free standing, or equally be placed on a three feet or metre-high plinth.

There is no formula for the successful mounting of carvings; only looking at pieces displayed in art galleries, shops, craft fairs or wherever they may be found will show you what works and what fails.

Projects Section

6 Torso

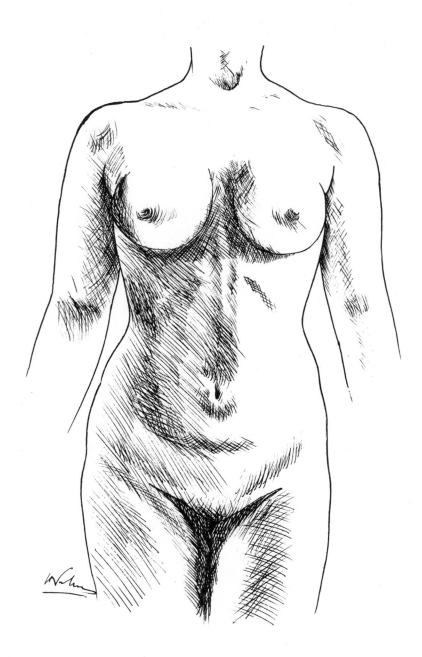

Figure 26

THERE is little point in carving anything without some objective over and above cutting wood. It would also seem rather pointless to attempt to make a perfect copy of a natural object since that is virtually doomed to failure. What is derisively called a "slavish imitation" of nature is more often a conscious or unconscious attempt to capture particular aspects of nature that have inspired the artist and to translate them into a medium. Somewhere between the inspiration and the translation, the genius of the artist, or lack of it, becomes apparent. As a carver you have a limited amount of room to manoeuvre—your ability to abstract qualities in nature is confined by your medium—wood. For instance, colour, unless you paint your carvings, is restricted; movement is limited; sound and smell are non-existent. The many effects that are posible for the painter, for example, the creation of space, air, and light; the 'movement' of bodies, clothes, animals, water, and so on; the atmospheres, attitudes and realisms—all these, at least most of these, are denied the woodcraftsman, although attempts have been made to create crowd scenes and landscapes. What you do have is form, texture, pattern and a few other more subtle qualities which you must use to advantage. The size and scale of the carving is important—very small carvings will never have the monumental qualities of a large one; larger than life-size figures will often have an unsatisfactory effect. There is no formula—it is what art is all about. The point is that the size of your carving must be considered, as must the type of timber, the grain and texture.

For the first project I have looked for a subject which is so well-known that everyone will be able to locate their own information source—the human body; to be precise, the female torso. Few subjects can have been more often portrayed. Study the paintings, drawings and sculptures, past and present, and observe the infinite variety of treatment. Ours must be simple, without detail and of a size that facilitates this first step into wood sculpture.

As a simple exercise into abstraction, the torso will be treated as a series of interlocking curved forms, the minor folds and dimples eliminated. It is not an attempt to create a life-like figure. Certain aspects have been emphasised, or inserted where they do not appear normally. For example the trunk is longer than in nature and some of the muscles and bones more strongly defined. This is a subjective decision which must be made by the individual.

A fairly strongly grained wood is needed to add variety to the large plain surfaces and to emphasize the shapes. An old beam of pitch pine was available, and although I normally avoid softwoods, I felt that for this simplified shape its bold grain would be ideal. Also its large dimensions would provide a fairly large carving, giving the rather statuesque impression I envisaged. If a large block is not available I think the use of unseasoned timber might be contemplated in this instance. After all, it is, perhaps, a first attempt and might end up as firewood. If the green timber is always kept in a sealed polythene bag whenever it is not being carved, it can be prevented from severe cracking. If when the actual carving is finished it is sanded and given several coats of polyurethane, a fairly good chance of it surviving unchecked is possible, provided it is kept away from dry atmospheres and heat. I have successfully done this with 6″ (152mm) diameter plumwood taken straight from a growing tree.

Design

The first step is to find your source of information. As you will find out, what you don't know about the human body is quite amazing. For the female torso in this project I used front back and side photos from a book on anatomy. These were quite small pictures so they had to be enlarged. This process is quite simple and will be used many times in the future. Simply draw a grid of lines at intervals, in this case 5mm, on the photos, then draw a similar grid with intervals of a suitably greater dimension in order to produce a picture the size you want for carving. Then copy the outline of the photo square by square onto your large grid. This will produce a fairly accurate drawing without any great skill. Do this for the front and side profiles. Now trace these profiles onto your block of wood on two adjacent faces. I find carbon paper easiest for this. Be sure that

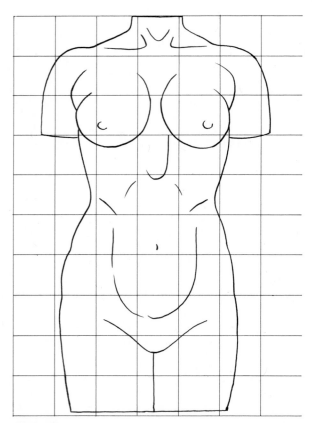

Figure 27

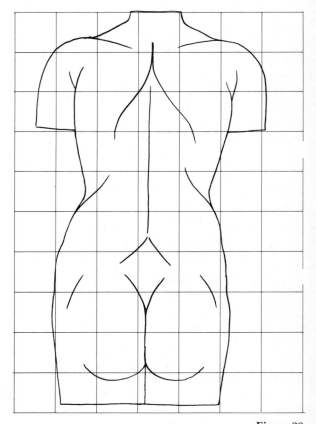

Figure 28

the drawings are exactly aligned on the block.

Bandsawing

The block must now be bandsawn from two directions to cut out both profiles. First cut the side profile since it is fairly straight and the waste can be removed in one or two large pieces. When this is done, pin the waste back on the block thereby replacing the front profile drawing. It must be stressed that these drawings be very accurate in relation to each other and very precisely positioned on the block. Any misalignment will be disastrous. This can now be bandsawn and all the waste removed. The result

will be a rather square, deformed, torso —but definitely recognisable. You now have fixed points of reference to work with in conjunction with your drawings; accurate measurements can be made, areas to be removed, determined. This is the importance of bandsawing. Parts of your carving are in precisely their finished position, therefore their relationship to the rest can be established with precision. The cut must be just on the line or just on its outside edge and the blade must be square in all directions and sharp. A bow saw might be used, but I find them inaccurate, arduous and limited in size. This system of band sawing will be used throughout the projects in this book. Occasionally it will be possible to cut from the top as well. A simple example is shown in Fig. 30, 31 and 32.

The block has been bandsawn and as can be seen in Fig. 33 the basic shape of the torso is quite well defined. The main areas of waste have been marked in. The extension of the legs is left since it is useful for holding in the vice. The first areas to be removed are the corners between the stumps of the arms and the

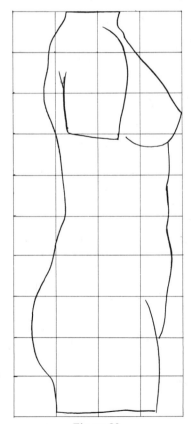

Figure 29

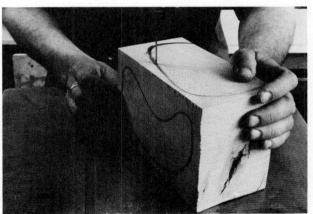

Figure 30

Figure 31

Figure 32

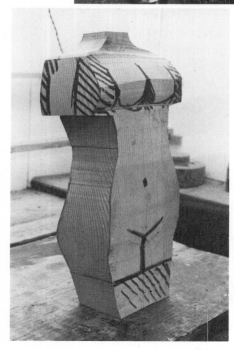

Figure 33

chest and back. A ½″ (12mm) No. 7 is used to chop out these areas. I use a mallet when roughing out a carving or making deep cuts on detail, for instance, cutting the division between the lips on the portrait or the undercutting of the hairline. Hand pressure is used more for shaving or paring work such as shaping the lips. Some carvers use the mallet virtually all the time whilst others replace it with the heel of the hand. This practice, however, was held responsible in the past for a condition amongst wood carvers in which the hand assumed a permanent claw-like position due to damaged tendons.

Care must be taken to avoid cutting against the grain wherever possible. Wood cuts easily with the grain, but splits and tears against it. If the lines of the grain are compared to the contour lines on a relief map, then you must always try to cut *down hill*. Fig. 34. The

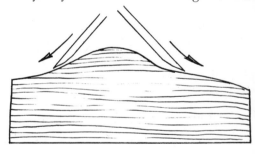

Figure 34

flatter ½″ (12mm) No. 3 is used to make the division between the legs and breasts. Cut across the grain rather than along it. Although this may not produce so clean a cut, it avoids the gouge following the grain and splitting off long slivers of wood. Fig. 35.

The next stage is to round off all the corners using the ½″ (12mm) No. 7. This

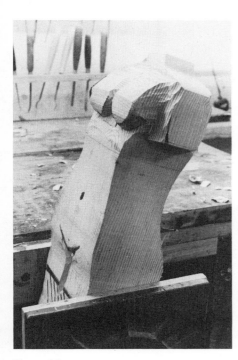

Figure 35

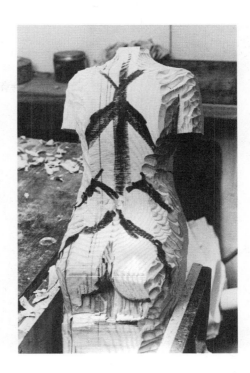

Figure 36

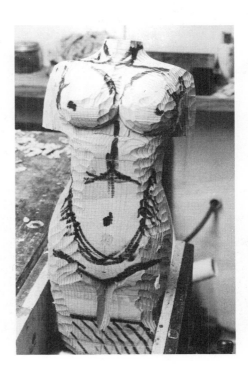

Figure 37

should result in an appearance somewhat like Figs. 36 and 37. The main masses of the anatomy can now be marked onto the wood—the spine, shoulder blades, buttocks, breasts etc., and more precisely shaped still with the ½″ (12mm) No. 7, resulting in the more lifelike shape of Fig. 38.

Now re-mark the carving with the outlines of the main masses, as shown in Figs. 39 and 40. It is not completely realistic, but a slight exaggeration of the shapes to be seen in nature. The buttocks are strongly defined as are the breasts. The shoulder blades are brought from the top of the shoulder in the spine and round to link up with the hips, which then swoop down around the belly. The crease of the groin makes a perfect "Y" shape with the legs. The breasts curl round and run into the collar bones. The

Figure 38

Figure 39

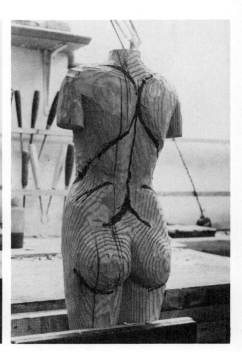

Figure 40

Figure 41

Figure 42

Figure 43

Figure 44

Figure 45   **Figure 46**

shape of the rib cage makes a shallow flat depression sloping down to the belly. The spinal groove is deeply cut and divides at the bottom of the back above the triangular pad characteristic of the female. The fatty area of the flank falls between the line of the hips and the buttocks. A ½″ (12mm) No. 9 will be necessary to cut in these main lines and the ½″ (12mm) No. 3 for incising the sharp folds such as under the breasts and arms. Figs. 41 and 42.

Figs. 43 and 44 show the torso virtually finished. The final definition of the form relies on the surface finishing to become more apparent. A sanded finish will make them more distinct than a tooled finish.

Figs. 45 and 46 show the basic technique of creating a tooled finish. In Fig. 45 the surface is deeply scalloped by the

½″ (12mm) No. 7 gouge which is being used to shape the shoulder.

In Fig. 46 these gouge marks are flattened using the ½″ (12mm) No. 3. This leaves a surface of concave facets, which, if the gouge cutting edges are sharp, should be clean and polished. This process can be continued, producing more flatter facets until the forms can be read accurately and a pleasing surface result. This surface should not be touched with any abrasive, but simply finished with oil or wax.

I personally felt a finely sanded and polished finish would be more sympathetic to the subject and more pleasing in appearance, so the torso was filed, sanded and finally sealed and wax polished as can be seen in the finished carving Fig. 47.

Figure 47

Tools used
for this project

½″ (12mm) No. 7 gouge
½″ (12mm) No. 3 gouge
½″ (12mm) No. 9 gouge

Bench vice
Files
Abrasives
Bandsaw

Timber: Pitch Pine
17″×8″×5″
(429mm×202mm×126mm)
Time: 3 days

7 Sting-ray

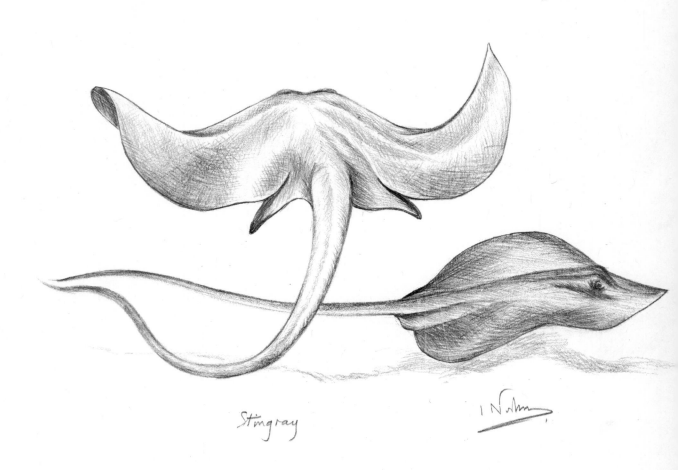

Stingray

Figure 48

TO carve a familiar object such as the torso is essentially a matter of observation, measurement and judicious removal of waste material. To do the same to a totally unfamiliar creature, such as a sting-ray, is not so simple. This is a freely designed interpretation and thus gives the carver a considerable latitude and freedom of expression. At the same time he must be aware of his intentions from the start and throughout so as not to lose his way during the abstraction of such a piece; and when he finds the form he requires it should be drawn-out in plan form just as any other work would be. There are innumerable examples of this approach in modern sculpture and some extremely beautiful pieces have been created as a result. Arguably, even the most faithful rendering of nature is a gross abstraction, as I have pointed out before.

In the case of the sting-ray I was very struck by this extraordinary fish's shape and motion; at the same time it seemed like a good exercise in carving the thin shapes of the wings and the long delicate tail. The timber used was rose zebrano, and with its pink colour and strong crimson lines, I felt that an exotic timber suited this peculiar fish. This carves well being fairly soft and cuts cleanly and easily, although the reader may wish to use any strikingly figured wood to bring out the flowing lines of this subject.

Draw the top and side views of the sting-ray and transfer the top view to the wood. Cut out the shape of the fish's body on the bandsaw, leaving it firmly attached to the plank by the thickest part of the tail, Fig. 50. Mark in the main areas to be removed on the upper surface. This consists of two deep channels either side of the body. Use a ½" (12mm) No. 9 gouge. This should leave the wood looking like Fig. 51. Now mark in the waste on the underside that is the wedge shaped pieces under the upturned end of each

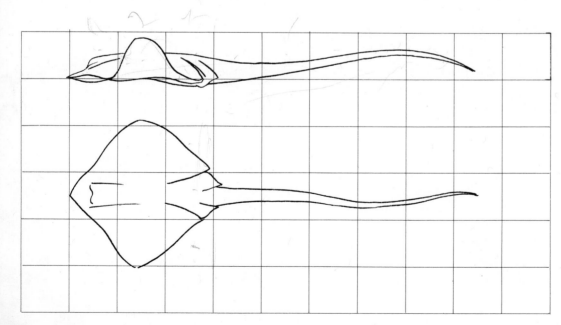

Figure 49

Figure 50

wing leaving about ¼″ (6mm) thickness at the wingtip. Also mark in the area to be cut away at the front of the head to form the front fin.

A fair degree of caution must be exercised removing the waste under the wings. Work from the wing-tip inwards towards the body, being careful to cut down-hill on the grain. The carving should appear as in Fig. 52. Now using a small gouge ¼″ (6mm) No. 9, cut in along the side of the body on the upper surface, and then with a ½″ (12mm) No. 3 lower the body below the level of the wing tips. Carefully begin to smooth out the upper surface and refine the shapes making them undulating and flowing. Figs. 53 and 54.

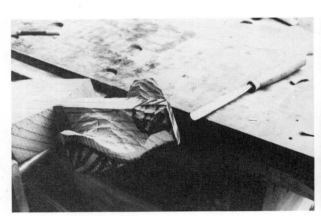

Figure 51

Figure 52

Figure 53

Figure 54

Turning the carving over on to its back refine the shape on the underside. Thin down and smooth the wing-tips first, hollowing them somewhat, and reducing them to about ⅛″ (3mm) thick at the thinnest point. Hollow the belly of the fish and cut a furrow either side of the body. Fig. 55. The tail can be initially shaped and the two small fins at the rear of the wings, cut in. Fig. 56.

The body should be filed and sanded at this point, since it is obviously safer and easier to do so while still attached to the plank, Now mark in the tail on the plank and bandsaw it out, Fig. 57, and then draw the side view of the tail on the resultant thin flat strip. Bandsawing this piece is not easy but can be achieved by resting the tail on a waste block so that the wings clear the table, and cutting through the tail and block together. You should now have a sting-ray with a square section tail. Fig. 58.

I did most of the shaping of the tail using a drum sander, vertically mounted in a chuck. The areas close to the body which this would not reach were carefully shaved down with a knife. The tail was then sanded and the whole fish given a coat of shellac sealer and subsequently rubbed down and waxed.

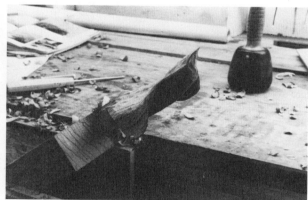

Figure 55

Figure 56

Figure 57

Figure 58

Figure 59

Tools used
for this project

½″ (12mm) No. 9 gouge
¼″ (6mm) No. 9 gouge
½″ (12mm) No. 3 gouge

Bench vice
Knife
Files
Drum sander
Abrasives

Timber: Rose Zebrano
20″×6″×2½″
(508mm×152mm×63mm)
Time: 2 days

8 Toad

Natterjack Toad!

Ian Nathan

Common Toad

Figure 60

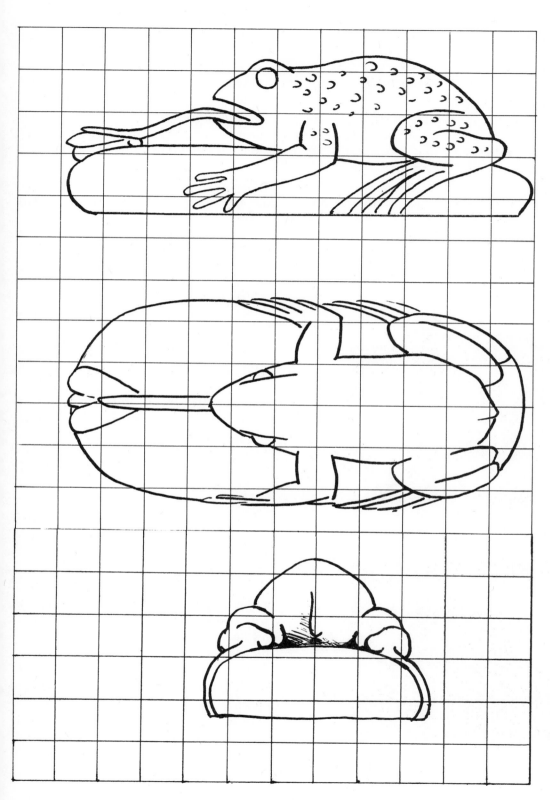

Figure 61

THIS little toad is an excuse to demonstrate the ukibori technique used by Japanese netsuke carvers. As a technique, it requires practice like anything else. In principle it consists of compressing the wood fibre at a given point to form a depression, levelling the surrounding wood until the depression disappears and then wetting the compressed area to swell it up again, thus creating a bump. I find it useful for odd little details such as the irregularity and knottiness of veins on a horse or an arm or leg, which it reproduces most convincingly.

Figure 62

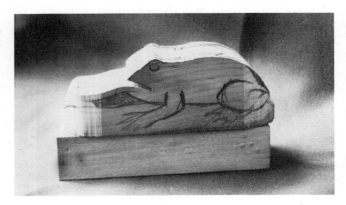

Figure 63

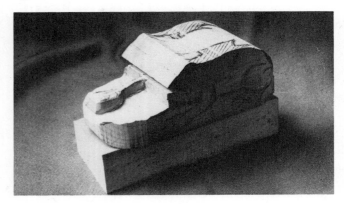

There is nothing particularly remarkable about ukibori except that it is a simple, obvious technique that is virtually unknown in this country. The object of the exercise is to make you think about different approaches to carving; different answers to problems. Texture, for instance, tends to be ignored. In the past, punches of many different types were used for textures, one german panel displaying the use of twenty-five different types.

Experimentation with different woods, tools, techniques, finishes and so on will expand your horizon as a carver and enable you to create effects that cannot be done by traditional methods.

The toad is simplified to a fair extent, and wrapped around a smooth oval pebble, his long tongue flicked out to catch a large fly.

The side profile can be drawn on the block and bandsawn. The round corners of the pebble can then easily be sawn off without recourse to further drawing. Screwed to a scrap block of wood it can be easily held in a bench vice, Fig. 62. In Fig. 63 the tongue and the fly have been isolated using a ¼″ (6mm) No. 9 and ½″ (12mm) No. 3. Do not undercut the tongue at this stage, so as to avoid breakage. The shape of the toad is drawn on the top and side surfaces, and using the ½″ (12mm) No. 3 cut down the sides to a slope as seen on the fore leg in Fig. 64. Then cut into the angle between the foreleg and the head, and the foreleg and the hindleg. Try to make the toolwork clean and tidy; on small carvings there is no room to do messy gouge-work and inaccurate cuts.

In Fig. 65 the pebble has been rounded off and the hind legs cut in between the elbows, back and pebble. All the legs and feet are now standing clear of the pebble and the toad is ready for shaping. In Fig. 66 the body and limbs have been rounded and undercut using ¼″ (6mm) No. 3—the pebble has been refined in the course of doing this and the tongue has been undercut. Mark the toes, eyes and the fly on the wood. Cut in the lines of the toes using a ⅛″ (3mm) V tool. In Fig. 67 the eyes are started by using a half round gouge, held vertically, and rotating it thus cuts a circle. This gradually cuts into the wood. The waste around the eye

can be removed leaving a low disc standing proud.

The disc is then carefully rounded using the inside curve of a ¼″ (6mm) No. 3. Notice that the eyes are slightly hooded. The wedge shape of the fly has been formed and the toes rounded. The area to be covered in warts is marked with black lines in the illustration Fig. 68. A punch is then prepared from a piece of steel rod—a nail will do. It must be ground to a hemisperical end and highly polished. In fact two different sizes were used on the toad ⅛″ (3mm) and ³⁄₁₆″

Figure 64

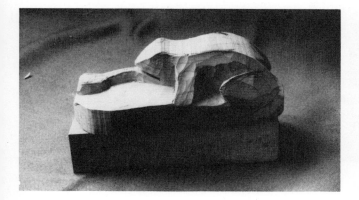

Figure 65

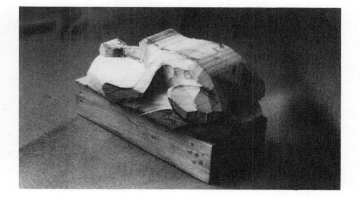

Figure 66

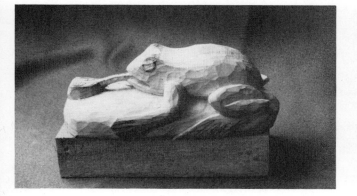

Figure 67

Figure 68

Figure 69

Figure 70

(5mm). The punch is tapped into the wood with a hammer. Experiment on waste wood before doing it. You will see that if it is driven in too deeply the wood punctures and crumbles. Practise this well until you are able to indent the wood every time (rather than puncture it) otherwise the surface will break away when the lumps are raised. Having completed the punching, Fig. 69, finish the fly, tongue, toes etc., and clean up any untidy toolcuts. Then carefully pare down all the punched area until the depressions have virtually gone. Then sand the whole carving very thoroughly.

Now, using a small paint brush and boiling water soak all the punched area. Within minutes the warts will be seen to rise, Fig. 70, and it will be observed that the degree of swelling and the damage to the wood is variable. In most instances of natural subjects this is not only acceptable but advantageous. It could be a problem, however, if one wished to imitate a man-made surface such as jewellery or studs of some sort.

Finally the toad is given a coat of potassium bichromate solution, which turns the yew wood a dark red-brown, followed by two coats of shellac sealer. I rubbed down with 000 grade steel wool and waxed polished, using a motorised brush. Fig. 71.

The little toad is a very simple but highly tactile object, made far more interesting by his warts. The prospect of carving them would have been daunting.

Figure 71

Tools used
for this project

¼″ (6mm) No. 9 gouge
½″ (12mm) No. 3 gouge
¼″ (6mm) No. 3 gouge
⅛″ (3mm) V chisel

Bench vice
Ukibori punches
Rifler files
Abrasives

Timber: English yew
6″×3″×2½″
(152mm×76mm×63mm)
Time: 1½ days

9 Portrait Head

Figure 72

Figure 73

Figure 74

IT should be fairly easy to carve a human head, after all we ought to know enough about its shape. Unfortunately, however, this is not the case. The fact is that the infinite variety of human features opens the door to almost any malformation or mistake being incorporated into the face, and so highly tuned is our ability to criticise and assess the tiniest subtleties in its making that a portrait remains one of the greatest challenges to an artist.

Inevitably, it will become necessary to carve a face, whether for its own sake or as a part of a figure carving, so the project in this chapter is to shape a basic head, incorporating the minimum of features, such as are found on the face of a young girl. There is no attempt to convey expression or likeness.

The head can be bandsawn from two sides quite effectively, although it is clearer on a male head with short hair.

Draw the front and side views on the sawn block, Fig. 75. The sides of the front profile are the hair, so the face must be revealed by removing the waste area on each cheek as can be seen in Fig. 76, this has been achieved using a ½″ (12mm) No. 9. This can be continued down the sides of the neck to the shoulders. Comparing the block with a real head should make it immediately apparent where the rounding-off of the face, hair and neck must take place, using ½″ (12mm) No. 9.

Smooth down the tool marks using a ½″ (12mm) No. 3 and cut in the nose in the shape of a wedge, Fig. 77, and mark in the eye sockets and the eyes.

Using a ½″ (12mm) No. 3 cut down from the eyebrows to the bottom edge of the lower lid, this being a flat plane sloping into the head. Then cut upward from cheek to meet this cut at the lower eyelid. You have effectively removed a large chip of wood which is the basic shape of the socket. This can be seen in Fig. 78.

Figure 75

Figure 76

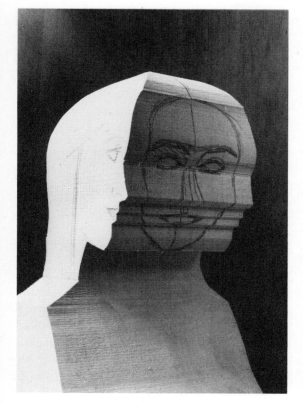

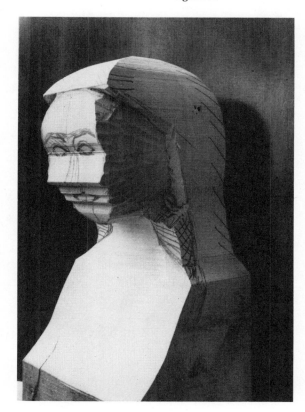

Figure 77

Figure 78

The cheeks can be blended into the sockets and the hairline undercut, then the shape of the face is generally refined. Remember to leave part of the earlobe protruding under the hair.

In Fig. 79 the left eye is shown partially complete to show what you are aiming at. First cut in the upper surface of the top lid using a ¾″ (19mm) No. 4—or a gouge that matches the curve of the lid; the inside curve of the gouge shaping the eyelid.

Next cut in the lower edge of the lower lid, in the same way, using ½″ (12mm) No. 3, and run ¼″ (6mm) No. 9 gouge under the lid to soften the cut, Fig. 80.

Now, using a ¼″ (6mm) No. 3, undercut the top and bottom lid forming the shape of the eyeball, which can then be rounded and smoothed off, Fig 81.

Figure 79

Figure 80

Figure 81

Figure 82

Refine the hollow under the lower lid using a ⅛″ (3mm) No. 9. Shape the socket above and below the eyelids. These shapes can be very subtle and it is in the formation of these areas that much of the eye's expression is found, rather than in the ball itself. The deep corners inside the lids are cut in with a small skew chisel or a knife.

Cut down the sides of the nose to form the ridge, and run a small gouge up the sides to the inner corner of the eye. Form the slightly winged undersides of the nostril and shape the upper lip. Using a ½″ (12mm) No. 7 cut down from the bridge of the nose towards the eye sockets.

The finer shapes of the nose must now be completed. Only constant reference to the real thing, by means of a mirror, can show you the delicate curves and hollows of a nose. Likewise the lips are too mobile and subtle to dictate a formula for carving, but I did most of the work with ¼″ (6mm) No. 3. Fig. 82 shows the face in the nearly finished state.

At this point, finish shaping the hair, neck and shoulders. In Fig. 83 this has been done and the face roughly filed and sanded. The shape can be carefully softened and altered using rifler and abrasives—there are very few edges on a girl's face. The hair was carefully tooled using ½″ (12mm) No. 2 and the result can

Figure 83

Figure 84

be seen in Fig. 84 ready for final sanding and polishing.

Should you wish to make the hair more lifelike there are many ways of doing so. Probably the easiest is to make numerous fine "V" tool cuts following the lines of the hair. On large areas however this can look rather overdone and the thin edges frequently crumble.

The best way I think, is to shape the main forms of the locks of hair, an example is shown in Fig. 85, and tool them to a smooth finish. Then make a series of cuts with a small 'U' shaped gouge, carefully following the curves of the hair. Follow this with similar cuts using an even smaller gouge. Do not overdo it, or the hair begins to look like straw.

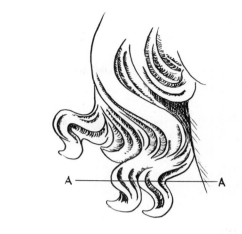

Figure 85

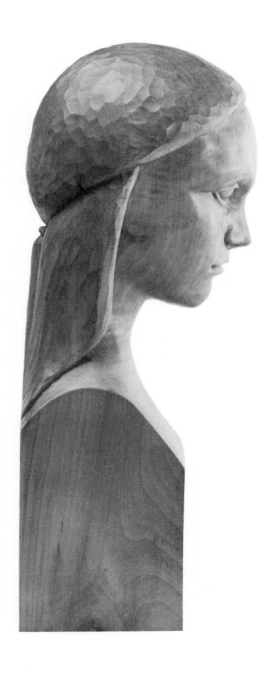

Figure 86

Tools used
for this project

½" (12mm) No. 9 gouge
½" (12mm) No. 3 gouge
¾" (19mm) No. 4 gouge
¼" (6mm) No. 9 gouge
⅛" (3mm) No. 9 gouge
½" (12mm) No. 7 gouge
½" (12mm) No. 2 gouge
¼" (6mm) skew chisel
¼" (6mm) No. 3 gouge

Bench vice
Rifler files
Abrasives

Timber: Limewood
6"×7"×15"
(152×178mm×381mm)
Time: 3 days

10 Horse's Head

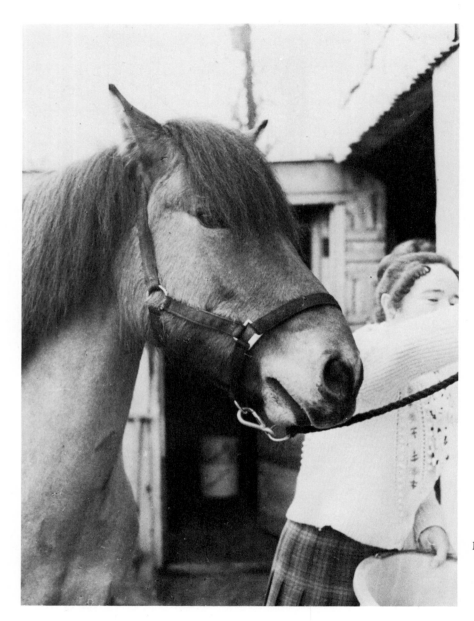

Figure 87

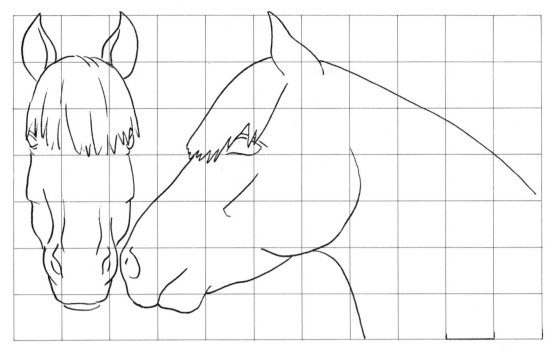

Figure 88

HORSES have never been more abundant or more popular. There is a wide variety of breeds and a great variation between individuals. They make excellent subjects for carving and have been favoured by sculptors since prehistoric times.

If you are thinking in terms of horses as portrait subjects for carving, bear in mind that horse owners are as critical of the results, if not more so, than are most people of human portraits. Consequently, if you want your carvings to be acceptable as a specific horse it must be very accurate. The particular pony in this project is a much loved pet and mount of the lady who commissioned his portrait.

The photograph of the horse is squared up and enlarged and the side profile is traced on to the block of wood. A few inches of waste wood is left on the neck to facilitate holding in the vice. The wood is then bandsawn to shape shown in Fig. 89. There is not much point bandsawing from the front profile as the shape is fairly flat, anyway.

Figure 89

The main features, the line of the jaw, the mane, the ears, eyes, mouth and so on, are drawn on the block.

Using a ½″ (12mm) No. 9 rough out the shape of the neck as shown in Fig. 90. It is thinner than the head and gets slimmer and more oval in section as it moves away from the head. Leave the mane raised up from the neck and head. Cut in around it with a flat gouge, ½″ (12mm) No. 3, Fig.

91, and cut away the waste between the ears and cut in the hair hanging over the face. This can be rounded-off as seen in the photographs. The eyes and the sharp bone running down the side of the cheek are the widest points of the face. The cheek, which is quite flat, must be cut down to a lower level than these points. The upper half of the face tapers from the cheek bone towards the ridge of the

Figure 90

Figure 91

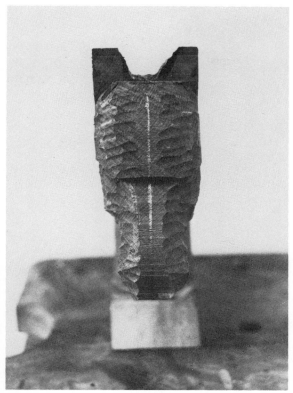

Figure 92

Figure 93

nose, Fig. 92. The bottom jaw tapers towards its lower side leaving the cheeks standing proud.

In Fig. 93 the shapes set out so far have been smoothed down using a ½″ (12mm) No. 3 and the main muscle formations have been marked on to the wood. These lines are cut in with a ½″ (12mm) No. 9,

Fig. 94, and blended in to form the subtle bone and muscle relief seen in the photographs. Following this cut in the mouth and shape the throat. Careful study of horse anatomy is the only way to be sure of what you are doing.

The line of the hair can now be marked in, Fig. 95. Cut in the lines of the mane,

Figure 94

Figure 95

Figure 96

Figure 97

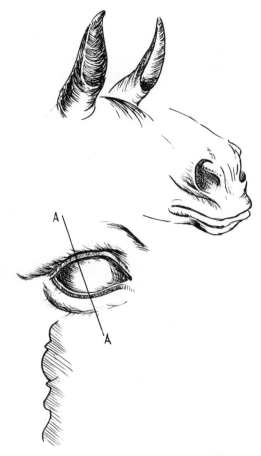

Figure 98

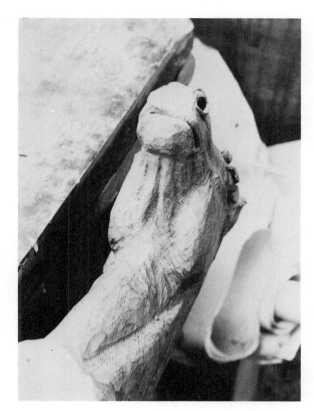

Figure 99

first with a ¼″ (6mm) V tool and then cutting the ends down to level of the body with the ½″ (12mm) No. 3 gouge. A small gouge, say a ¼″ (6mm) No. 3 may be needed to remove the waste. These clumps of hair are rounded-off and undercut to give the appearance of laying on top of the flesh, Fig. 96. The eyes can now be carved. This requires great care and especially sharp chisels. The horse's eye is in fact more complex than is shown here in Fig. 97, but the hair hanging over it makes it difficult enough. The nostrils can also be cut in

and the rest of the head more carefully tooled and finished. The ears can be hollowed slightly. It will be seen on a real horse, that the ears are in the form of tubes sliced off at an angle. They are filled with hair so I tend to compromise by partially hollowing them. If they are too thin they are sure to get broken.

Fig. 98 shows two different sketches of the ear, one more hollowed than the other, nostrils and mouth, and the eye when fully visible, without overhanging hair. They should be used only as a guide for the particular type of features you are trying to convey or copy.

The throat area and neck are quite straight forward and should not present any problem. Fig. 99 shows this stage almost completed.

Finally, the hair of the mane is textured. This pony has a heavy coarse mane, and I felt the right feel would be achieved by numerous irregular tool cuts. Many cuts were put in first with a ¼″ (6mm) No. 9 and these were then overlaid by yet more cuts with ⅛″ (3mm) No. 9, Fig. 100. The coarse grain of oak will let you down at this point by crumbling on the thin cross grain edge if particular attention is not paid to sharpness and grain direction. Also the sequence of cuts is important. If two gouge cuts are made ¼″ (6mm) apart, a third cut between them is likely to result in crumbling of both adjacent edges. This would be less likely, if the cuts were made in sequence from one side to the other.

The head can now be carefully tooled, which is always attractive in oak, or sanded. I have sanded this one for the satisfaction of the customer. It was subsequently oiled and wax polished.

Mounting a horse's head presents a slight problem. If the neck is stretched out then it creates an imbalance on the base tending to be front heavy. However, if the all-over design is a diamond shape, as shown, it is more symmetrical. It can then be screwed to a plain square block of wood, in this case, white oak. I normally cover the bottom of the base with self-adhesive felt to protect furniture.

Figure 100

Figure 101

Tools used
for this project

½″ (12mm) No. 9 gouge
½″ (12mm) No. 3 gouge
¼″ (6mm) V chisel
¼″ (6mm) No. 3 gouge
⅛″ (3mm) No. 9 gouge
¼″ (6mm) No. 9 gouge

Bench vice
Rifler files
Abrasives

Timber: Brown oak
9″×7″×3″
(229mm×178mm×76mm)
Time: 2 days

11 Harlequin

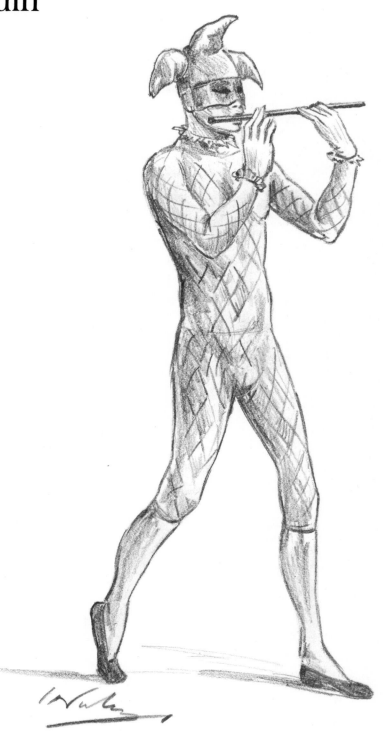

Figure 102

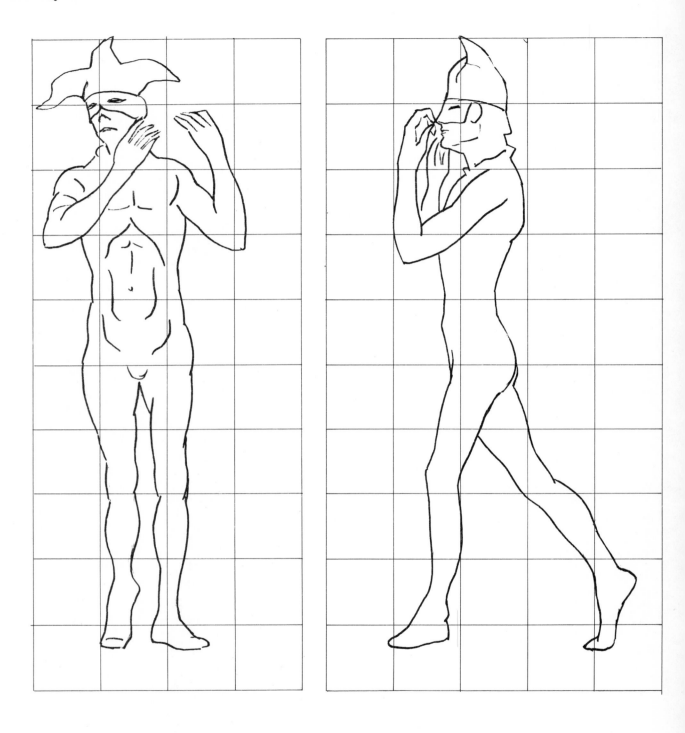

Figure 103

Figure 104

THIS project is designed as a simple exercise in carving a figure and understanding some of the problems involved. Apart from the purely technical ones, it must be remembered that the audience is able to be highly critical of any representation of the human body, since they are so thoroughly aquainted with it. Any slight imbalance, disproportion and unnaturalness will be picked out, consciously or unconsciously, by even the most sympathetic observer. The purpose of this carving, then, is to bring home this difficulty and prepare the carver for future more complex figures.

Harlequin is just the name of the character from the Italian Commedia Del Arte who traditionally wore the familiar patchwork clothes, a mask and a hat. His other characteristics have varied so much over the centuries that he is all things to all men. However, the figure I visualized is tall, very slim and must be as light as the music he plays on his flute. The timber is a very stripy English walnut.

Bandsaw the block, leaving the area between the legs untouched. This leaves the end of the block attached for holding in the vice and keeps the legs strong enough to withstand the force of the mallet. The piece should look like Figs. 105 and 106 after sawing. The waste between the legs is marked, and left, and

Figure 105

Figure 106

Figure 107

Figure 108

the waste between the two arms is marked and can be removed with a ¼″ (6mm) No. 9, along with the areas below the upper arms and within the fold of the forearm and upper arm. In Fig. 107 this work has been completed and cleaned up with a ½″ (12mm) No. 2. It is now necessary to put the required angles on to the arm by paring down the upper arms from elbow to shoulder.

In Fig. 108 the position of the arms is becoming clearer. What now needs removing is the excess on the chest, between the arms. This is cut away with the same gouge without difficulty, and at the same time the arms are freed and can be clearly seen in Fig. 109. Work can now commence on shaping the body. Mark the central line of the torso and the main anatomical features. The markings running down the corners in Fig. 109, indicate where the figure can be rounded-off, Reference to your own body is the obvious way to find shapes of the various limbs, and simply by rounding-off the corners your figure should soon look like Fig. 110.

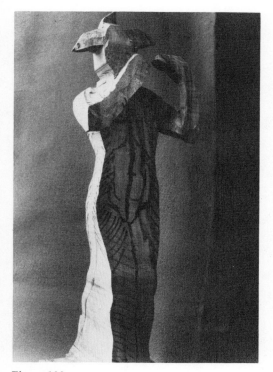

Figure 109

Figure 110

Figure 111

Fig. 111 shows that slightly more shaping has been completed in the back; the grooves down the spine and the buttocks have been roughly cut. The neck has been thinned down leaving the collar proud, the hat is shaping up. On the front, the main anatomical features have been roughly shaped and the arms separated from the face more, as the hand is shaped. This can be observed

Figure 112

Figure 113

in Fig. 112. The torso arms and head are ready to be detailed and the area between the legs cut away but with the feet still firmly attached.

In the final stages Fig. 113 the detail is carved in working down from the hat.

The mask is shaped like a face but ⅛″ (3mm) higher. The eyeholes were cut with ⅛″ (3mm) No. 2 and hollowed out with a dentist's drill in a flexi-shaft. This was used again to make the holes at the ends of the folds of the collar.

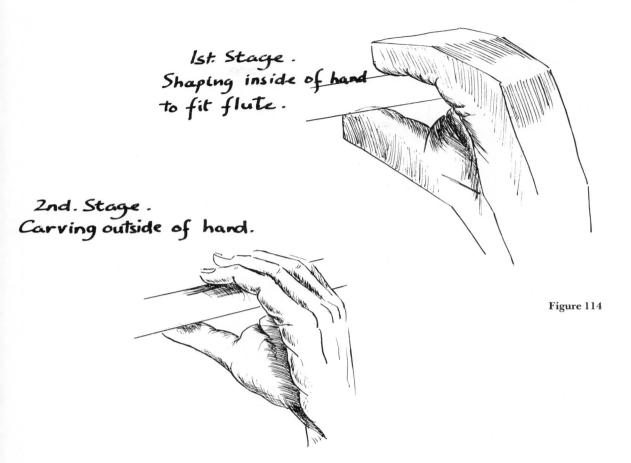

1st. Stage.
Shaping inside of hand
to fit flute.

2nd. Stage.
Carving outside of hand.

Figure 114

At this point the flute should be made, preferably on a lathe, so that the hands can be carved to fit it. The hands are difficult, because they are finely detailed, and also, once again, because they are highly criticizable. It is best to carve the inside-curve first, fit the flute, then carve the outer curve and cut in the fingers. Fig. 114 shows the two main stages. You will find that it is not only easier to carve the inside of the hand first but, in many cases essential, particularly when your intention is to line-up the hands with some other feature or object—in this case, the hands to the flute to the mouth. Most of this can be done with a ¼″ (6mm) No. 2, although both a sharp knife and the rotary burrs can be useful. The whole of the upper body and limbs should be carefully tooled before completing the legs and feet. Having done that, work down the legs, finally the feet and then cut the waste end of the block. The last task before finishing, is to carefully glue the flute into position.

Linseed oil will now bring up the grain beautifully in the walnut.

Figure 115

Tools used
for this project

¼″ (6mm) No. 9 gouge
½″ (12mm) No. 2 gouge
⅛″ (3mm) No. 2 gouge
¼″ (6mm) No. 2 gouge

Bench vice
Flexi-shaft & burrs
Knife

Timber: English walnut
3¼″×4″×12″
(83mm×101mm×305mm)
Ebony: ¼″×¼″×3″
(6mm×6mm×76mm)
Time: 2 days

12 Still Life

Figure 116(a)

Figure 116(b)

I FOUND this still life quite fascinating to carve and an excellent exercise. The Emmental cheese was disgracefully expensive and in view of its mediocre flavour and waxy texture I was not sorry to see it dry up and be consigned to the bin.

It is not my intention that you should copy the still life I have carved. Indeed, all the projects in this book are guides to a method of working rather than subjects for imitation. It should be no trouble for anyone to set up an arrangement of objects to carve, and in this case we are attempting to imitate nature, so the objects must be chosen with care. For example, a bone would be fine, whereas a slice of bread could be extremely difficult. It would probably be a good idea to try copying a few articles separately before commencing a group.

There is an immense amount of knowledge about shapes and textures and an oddly satisfying surrealistic quality to be gained from this type of carving. It is at once very easy and very difficult. The problems of knowing what shape to carve, what dimensions, forms, etc., are completely eliminated but the technical problems of duplicating the shape so clearly before you, cannot be avoided; and to look good the replica must be accurate.

It will be observed in the photographs Fig. 116 of my original still life there is a burnt match. I left this off the carving as I felt that without its burnt quality it would be difficult to distinguish that it was in fact a match, underlining the point made earlier with regard to the choice of suitable subjects.

The still life was carefully measured and drawn life size onto the sides of a block of limewood, Fig. 117, then bandsawn from both sides resulting in the odd shape seen in Fig. 118. The obvious areas of waste are marked: the "extra" knife handle and candle flame and the large wedge running parallel to the cheese, also the piece to the right of the candle corresponding to the apple. These can quickly be removed with ½" (12mm) No. 9 and ½" (12mm) No. 2. In Fig. 119 the

Figure 117

Figure 118

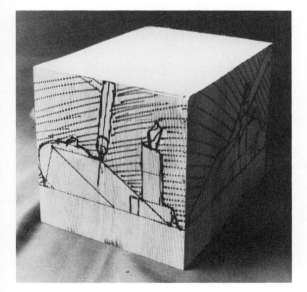

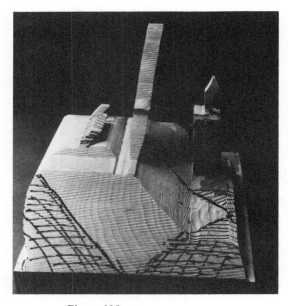

Figure 119

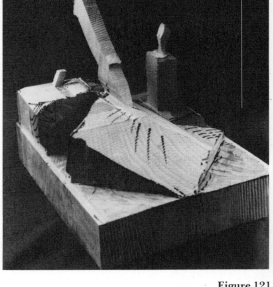

Figure 121

candle is now isolated and it can be seen that there is a piece to be removed adjoining the apple stem, and the large areas around the cheese can be cut away to form the marble slab which it is supposed to be on.

In Fig. 120 this has been completed. The waste between the segment of apple and the apple, the piece in front of the segment, and the area between the apple and the cheese are all marked for re-moval. Fig 121 shows this accomplished and the set up is taking shape although everything is still square and the cheese has a peculiar pyramidal upper surface, which must be flattened. The apple must be converted from a cube to a cylinder. This can be seen in Fig. 122. Also the segment is now wedge shaped and the cheese has a flat surface.

Fig. 123 shows the result of very careful paring of the flat surface with ½″ (12mm)

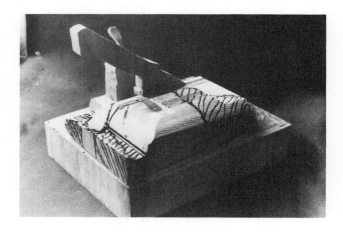

Figure 120

Figure 122

No. 2 and a ¾″ (19mm) No. 1. Also the candle has become cylindrical and the matchbox cut in. The knife has acquired some shape as a necessity of flattening the cheese. Also the entire surface of the marble slab has been exposed. Considerable use of a ¼″ (6mm) No. 3 spoon bent gouge is necessary to achieve the flattening of the area in the middle of the objects. The flattening of surfaces is almost complete in Fig. 124 and the apple has been made into a sphere. The segment has been shaped and the run of candle wax roughly carved in.

At this point you could sand the main surfaces: the apple, segment, candle, matchbox, cheese and slab. The knife, apple stalk and flame were left relatively untouched and fairly robust, Fig. 125.

Having achieved a finish on these areas the fine details could now be carved. The holes in the cheese were cut with a ¼″ (6mm) No. 7 and ¼″ (6mm) No. 2. The edges around the matchbox were incised with a knife. The melted candle wax was shaped with a ¼″ (6mm) No. 2 and finished with rifler files, and the space for the section of apple removed with a 1″ (25mm) No. 1. The knife is carved working from the end of the handle downwards, maintaining the

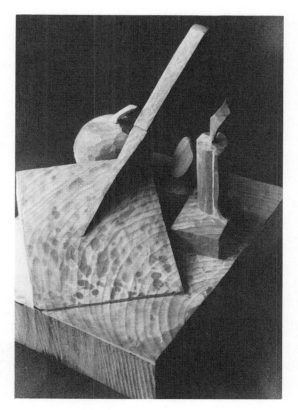

Figure 124

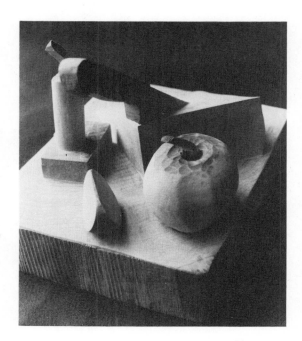

Figure 125

Figure 123

strength of the blade for as long as possible, Fig 126. At this point I found that I could not get the smoothness I wanted in the deep depression in the top of the apple, so I broke off the stalk and later replaced it by gluing. This adaptability and experimentation on the part of the carver should prevail throughout any exercise and with any subject. Gluing extra pieces of wood to accommodate length, change, finishing, etc., are all part and parcel of what creative carving should be. Another example would be if,

say, the top centre part of the apple segment broke away through careless tooling or grain fault, the carver could create this 'upset' into a possible advantage by having a segment with a bite into it—and so on.

It only remained to cut the final hole in the cheese which is bisected by the knife blade, and to finish the candle flame. Sanding must be extremely thorough to achieve the maximum visual impact of an object, apparently familiar, yet in a totally alien material.

Figure 126

Figure 127

Tools used for this project

½″ (12mm) No. 9 gouge
½″ (12mm) No. 2 gouge
¾″ (19mm) No. 1 Chisel
¼″ (6mm) No. 7 gouge
¼″ (6mm) No. 2 gouge
1″ (25mm) No. 1 chisel
¼″ (6mm) No. 3 spoonbent

Bench vice
Rifler files
Abrasives

Timber: Limewood
9″×7″×6″
(229mm×178mm×152mm)
Time: 4 days

13 Black Bull

Figure 128

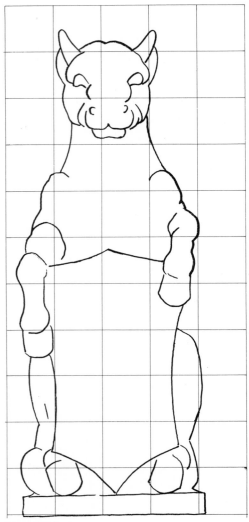

Figure 129

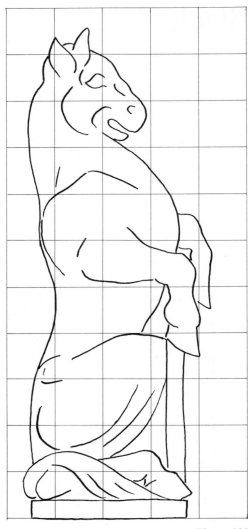

Figure 130

HERALDRY began in the early medieval period in the form of simple, bold, brightly coloured symbols carried by armoured knights and their followers, as a means of identification. Since then it has become a 'science' dealing with complex family trees and elaborate coats of arms. These are issued by the College of Heralds to all manner of individuals and organisations for a wide variety of reasons. Heraldry is a living, thriving anachronism and one which can provide the carver with a rich and varied source of inspiration, and probably the easiest source of financial remuneration, for it is still fairly common for heraldic devices in various media to be commissioned from artists and craftsmen.

Heraldic beasts were generally employed for some quality attributed to them—strength, ferocity, magical powers—and they may be mythical, such as the griffon and wyvern, or real, like the lion or, in this case, the bull. His attributes are pretty obviously, brute strength and fierceness, and they must be borne in mind at all times, since they are the object of the exercise, so to speak. The bull is one of ten, made for a customer, based on the Queen's beasts at Hampton Court, Windsor Castle and Kew Gardens.

Figure 131

Figure 132

Figure 133

Figure 134

I chose to do the Bull in African Black-wood, a rather expensive, very hard wood, which, although better to carve than ebony is, nevertheless, difficult and very hard on the chisel. A few blows with the mallet will splinter the cutting edge, and often break off chunks of steel ⅛" (3mm) long from the corners. However, the beautiful satiny finish and brown-black and purple grain make it worth struggling with. The practising wood-carver may wish to choose an alternative and a fine-grained hardwood, such as pear or boxwood, could be used and then, if required, stained black.

Bandsaw the shape of the bull from two sides, taking care that the cut is square and straight; this will result in the shape shown in Fig. 131. Barrelling of bandsaw blades can be a problem when working with thick, hard woods which causes the blade to belly-out on the cutting line.

Mark in the main features and then the large areas of waste at the top of the shield and between the shield and the hind legs. This is hard work using black-wood and rotary burrs could be used to good effect. Try to cut the waste away cleanly to give you a clear idea of the shape. You should now have the figure as shown in Fig. 132. Mark in the waste area between the hind legs, fore legs and body so that the limbs begin to stand away from the chest and belly. Also, the area between the fore feet can be reduced so that the shield becomes flat. It is a good idea at this time to finish the surface of the shield completely so that you have a definite level to work to and can cut into the back of it accurately.

All the work so far, can be done with a ¼″ (6mm) No. 9 and ¼″ (6mm) No. 3.

The small markings down the rear edges in Fig. 133 signify corners to be rounded-off. In Fig. 134 this has been done, using knowledge of the bull's shape from reference material to suggest the form of the muscular shoulders and the thick tail. The V-shaped crease down the back can be cut in; its final shape is shown in Fig. 140.

Fig. 135 shows the bull with the line of the hind hoof and leg marked in, and lines showing where the hind leg, fore leg and chest can be rounded. Fig. 136 shows this shaping and work is about to start on the head.

Roughly shape the head, cutting in the horn and ears as shown in Fig. 137. Begin to put some shape into the fore hooves so

Figure 135

Figure 136

Figure 137

Figure 138

that the precise shape of the shield can be determined. The same can be done to the hind hooves, not forgetting the tail. In Fig. 138 the somewhat stylized creases of the body are marked along with the line of the jaw. Virtually all this rough work can be done using the two gouges men-tioned earlier. If the edges of the tools are spoilt by the blackwood, it is as well to limit the damage to as few as possible. Fig. 139 shows this work completed and a general cleaning up of the carving has been started. Only the head is still in the rough.

Before detailing the head and adding fine touches such as the hairs on the hooves and tail the whole carving is finely tooled, filed and partially sanded, Fig. 140. Files tend to clog rather quickly but blackwood scrapes extremely well. A carpenter's chisel, knife or sharpened piece of tool steel will be found to peel the wood easily and cleanly leaving a smooth polished surface.

The back of the shield should be undercut to a point where it is no longer obtrusive. There is about one inch of solid wood between the sides of the chest and the shield on my example, and the area between the hind legs is almost completely solid. If you feel it is necessary to remove this wood I suggest you use rotary burrs.

Fig. 141 shows the first stage in finishing the head. The cheeks have been cut in and rounded, and the bulging eye sockets set out above them. The ears and horns are clearly deliniated and the tufts of hair on the forehead which are left until last. The formation of the head is basically similar to that of the horse.

Figure 139

Figure 140

At this point you must consider your carving as a whole and decide whether you have captured the feeling of power and ferocity of the bull. After hours of sanding it will be disastrous to have to start carving again. The final details are incised using small gouges and scrapers, Fig. 142. The eyes are carved in the same way as the horse's Fig. 98, but the nostrils are virtually drilled holes, with folds cut in around them. The mouth can be cut with a modeller's or jeweller's saw. The deep folds and creases around the neck and chest can be cut and filed before sanding the whole carving. After fine sanding, to about 120 grit, the curls on the head and the tufts of hair round the hooves can be incised with a ⅛″ (3mm) V tool and the sanding completed with the very finest abrasives available. Only the lightest wax polishing will be necessary on blackwood and no sealer required.

Figure 141

Figure 142

Figure 143

Tools used
for this project

¼″ (6mm) No. 9 gouge
¼″ (6mm) No. 3 gouge
⅛″ (3mm) No. 9 gouge
⅛″ (3mm) V chisel

Bench vice
Knife
Dental scrapers
Rifler files
Coping saw
Abrasives

Timber: African blackwood
11″×4″×4″
(280mm×101mm×101mm)
Time: 6 days

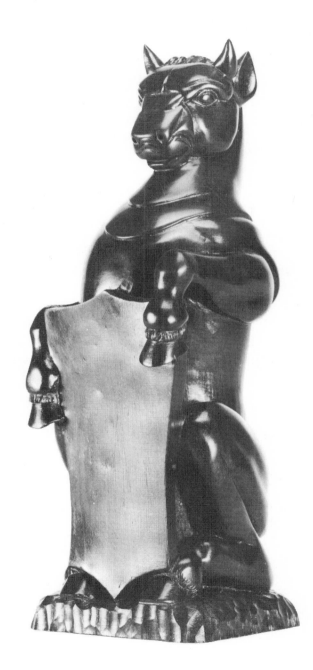

14 Greenland Gyr Falcon

Figure 144

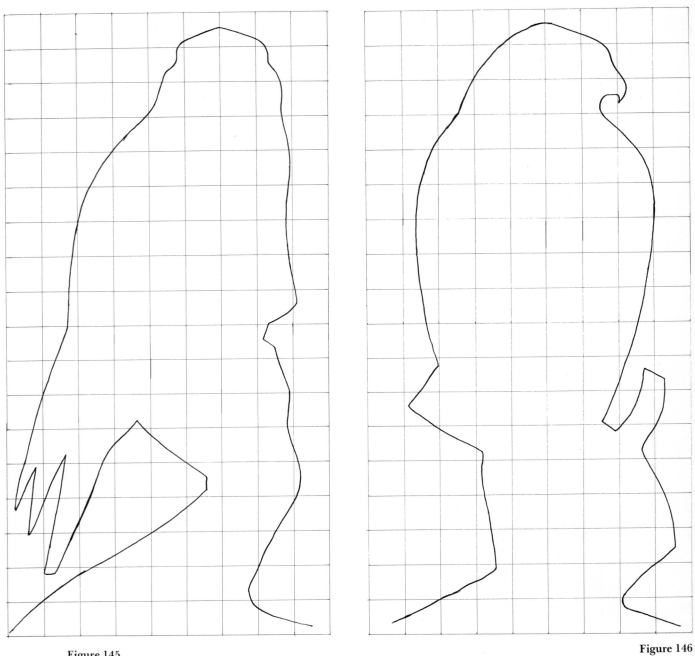

Figure 145

Figure 146

CARVING birds presents a number of problems which make the decision-making process almost of greater importance than the technical ones. Firstly, birds fly and wood does not — to capture flight in a sculpture would be an achievement indeed. Such devices as attaching a wingtip to the ground rarely work well although I have seen the work of an American who employs thin spring steel strips embedded in the wing tips and a branch to make the connection as small as possible; but I think as a whole, it always tends to look contrived.

Secondly, birds are cursed with extremely thin legs, which, when made from the solid wood block would hardly bear the body weight let alone withstand any vibration. Use has been made of metal, painted to look like wood, and again of support for the bird's body at a second point.

Thirdly, birds unfortunately are covered with innumerable feathers, which, in all the interesting poses, seem to take on the fluffiest, thinnest, most shapeless appearance they can, in a deliberate attempt to thwart woodcarvers and encourage painters!

Added to this is the fact that most birds tend to look the same when their colours cannot be seen. It falls on the carver to

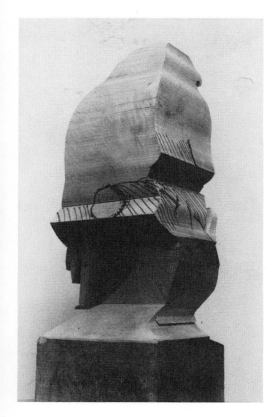

Figure 147

Figure 148

decide whether to carve the shape of the bird, or to carve in the feathers as well, or to carve the feathers and all the thousands of little lines that make up the feathers, for this has indeed been done especially by the Orientals, with staggering success. Personally, I am not prepared to devote a sizeable portion of my life proving that I know what feathers look like.

The bird is a three-dimensional form with certain associations; in the case of the bird of prey, they are powerful ones and well-known. One brings to mind the medieval sport of falconry, for which the gyr falcon was highly prized—the legendary speed of flight, the terrible claws and beak, and the incredible eyesight.

Bearing in mind the problems referred to earlier, I felt that brooding malevolence and potential power was the best image to aim for, and for the practising carver an excellent chance to bring about such characteristics.

The timber used was an 8″×8″ (203mm×203mm) block of sycamore which had lain unused for many years in a sawmill in the Cotswolds, and was bought for a tenth of its value. It turned out to be beautifully figured and virtually flawless except for a small dead knot which, unfortunately, fell right in the middle of the bird's chest.

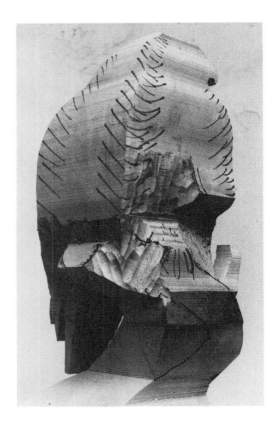

Figure 149

Figure 150

Figure 151

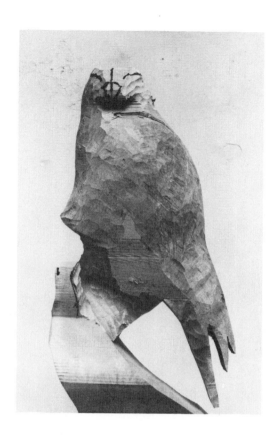

Figure 152

The falcon was drawn originally from a book on birds, and a considerable amount of research done in books and in the stuffed bird department of the local museum. I found the areas of feathers and main shapes of the body to be very poorly defined and variable. The most important aspect here is that the carver should be guided by his reference material, (whether photograph or three-dimensional study) and carefully define those features which typify the bird's form.

Having drawn the profiles on the front and side of the block and bandsawn it, the result is seen in Fig. 147. I have marked on the block the waste area extending left from the curled up foot. Also the areas to the front and rear of the main branch, leaving plenty of space round the left claw. Fig. 148, shows the rear view and waste extending from the small branch backwards and down the side of the tail. All this is removed with a ½″ (12mm) No. 9.

Fig. 149 shows the waste removed and the figure marked where the corners can be rounded off. In Fig. 150 this has been completed on the main body and the head and tail can be treated in the same way. The basic shape of the bird is now beginning to emerge as shown in Fig. 151.

Figure 153

Figure 154

The main body can now be tooled to a fairly smooth finish, Fig. 152, using a ½″ (12mm) No. 3, so that the basic form can be clearly seen. The head is now marked with a centre line, showing the approximate position of the beak and furrows down each side of the head in which the eyes lie. Also the branch can be rounded and the claws isolated. Fig. 153 shows this stage completed. The head is shaped and tooled to a smooth finish using a ¼″ (6mm) No. 9 and ¼″ (6mm) No. 2. The branch has been roughed out and the body cut in around it, and the position of the claw clarified. The feathers have been parted on the chest and a lump left

for the curled claw. The branch has been left quite solidly attached to the under-side of the tail to maintain strength. It is interesting to note that at this point the dead knot in the chest has appeared, whereas previously it was not apparent.

Faults in wood create something of a quandary for the carver. If the fault is obvious before beginning to carve then it is really unforgivable to use the wood and apologise for the blemish after-wards. If the fault appears during the process of carving, as often happens, then it must be decided whether it affects the structure of the carving, and if not whether it will be acceptable as a natural feature of the wood. A small dead knot or crack might be filled with coloured wax, filler, or simply left, assuming it is not, for instance, in the middle of the eye or lips. Severe defects such as those on the torso may warrant abandoning the piece, although in this case I felt that the strong grain, and the fault being on the back, would carry it off. What you should almost never do, in my opinion, is try to repair the fault by cutting it away and inserting in a new piece of wood. This will immediately give the carving a 're-paired' appearance and invite the suggestion that you made a mistake.

The bulk of the shaping of feathers is found at the back of the bird and Fig. 154 shows the main groupings marked in as the tail, the wingtips and the centre of the back. The waste round the tail and wings can be cut away with a ½" (12mm) No. 3 and the central crease and wing sides put in with a ¼" (6mm) V tool. Fig. 155 shows this completed. The wing tips and tail can now be undercut and tooled to a smooth finish and the subtler feathers on the back and side which descend down the body in tiers, and the upper ones overlaying the lower, in circular shape are marked in Fig. 156.

Figure 155

Figure 156

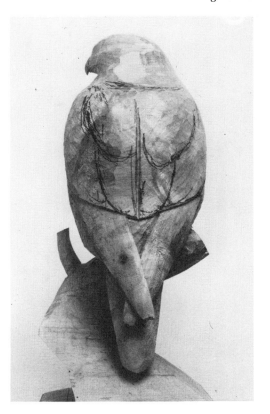

I cut these feathers in using a ¼″ (6mm) macaroni tool, but a V tool could be used. These are then rounded-off and smoothed, Fig. 157. The beautiful figuring of the wood is now beginning to show in the piece of sycamore I chose. If you happen to discover at a specific point in any project when the grain or figure in the wood comes through particularly strongly then it in many cases provides one with the opportunity to perhaps reconsider treatment of the subject.

Turning to the front of the falcon, mark in the collar-type feathers below the head and the two grooves running down either side of the chest, Fig. 158. These are not the wings, but very soft downy feathers that appear to overlay the front edge of the wings, effectively concealing them. The claw on the branch can be cut in as shown; firstly, cutting away the waste between the claws using a ¼″ (6mm) No. 2 and carrying the surface of the branch between the claws. Then

Figure 157

Figure 158

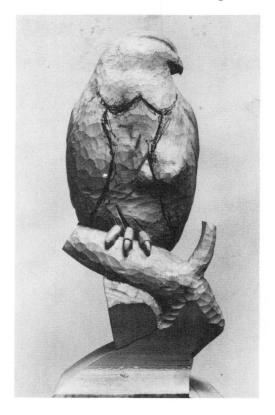

Figure 159

Figure 160

using the same chisel, round-off the claws into a sausage like shape. Now carefully cut into the sausage, about a third along its length and leave a thinner section for the talon. Fig. 158 shows two claws completed to this stage.

Fig. 159 shows the collar and the two side grooves cut and shaped. The claws can be seen, the talons now partially undercut using a ¼" (6mm) No. 5. This undercutting must be attacked from both sides until you break through. The inside curve of the talon can then be finished with a riffler or needle file. Finally, refine the outside surfaces of the talon. They are very delicate.

Work can now begin on the head. Fig 160 shows the beak and adjoining feathers marked and the leading edge of the eye sockets.

Figure 161

The completed head is shown in Fig. 161. The eyball has been cut in by carefully rotating a small gouge of the appropriate curvature, in this case a ¼" (6mm) No. 5. This leaves a small cylinder which is carefully rounded and smoothed. Then cut the small ring around the eyeball by the same method and undercut the brow with a ⅛" (3mm) No. 9 gouge. Cut in the groove running from the beak under the eye with a V tool and blend it into the area round the eye with a ¼" (6mm) No. 2.

The beak is formed using a ¼" (6mm) No. 2 cutting back toward the fold of skin above the beak and chopping in around the line of the latter to isolate the shape of it. Refine it down until it is suitably sharp and nasty looking, then cut in the wavy line which separates the upper and lower

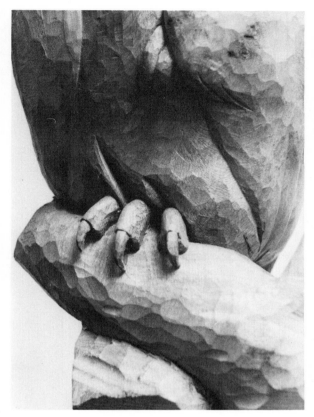

Figure 162

Figure 163

halves. Now you can form the grooves running from below the beak down the sides of the neck.

Only thorough reference to a real falcon's head will result in true accuracy, but personally, I found the real thing not nearly as impressive as I had expected and I preferred to emphasise certain aspects of the falcon in order to create the powerful image I had originally conceived. This, obviously, is a matter of choice for the individual carver.

Once the head is completely finished the other major detail is the claws. Fig. 162 shows the claws finished but for the scales and the pads. Deep incisions have been cut where they part the feathers. The scales can now be cut using a ¼" (6mm) No. 2 chopping down vertically on the line of each scale, and paring back towards the cut, Fig. 163. The spaces between the pads are then removed with a ¼" (6mm) No. 5. Very careful undercutting is necessary to give separation from the branch. A little more feathering is added to the area displaced by the curled foot.

Decision time again regarding the branch. If it were carved in imitation of a real branch it would be completely out of keeping with the very simplified falcon. On the other hand, I felt it needed a contrast with the smooth finish of the bird. Finally I decided on a coarsely tooled finish, but bear in mind, this must be quite carefully done. The final separation of the branch from the bird can be completed and the underside of the tail carefully tooled, Fig. 164.

To finish the bird, very careful tooling of the whole surface, requiring a re-sharpening of the necessary gouges to a razor edge. Simply, try to get the surface as smooth as possible, then wipe over it with linseed oil. Any defects, chisel cuts, tears, etc., will show up and can be removed. Leave the oil to dry for a few days, rub down with fine steel wool and wax polish.

Figure 164

Figure 165

Tools used
for this project

½″ (12mm) No. 9 gouge
½″ (12mm) No. 3 gouge
¼″ (6mm) No. 9 gouge
¼″ (6mm) No. 2 gouge
¼″ (6mm) V chisel
¼″ (6mm) No. 5 gouge
⅛″ (3mm) No. 9 gouge
¼″ (6mm) Macaroni tool

Bench vice
Rifler files

Timber: Sycamore
8″×8″×18″
(203mm×203mm×457mm)
Time: 5 days

15 The Caterpillar

Figure 166

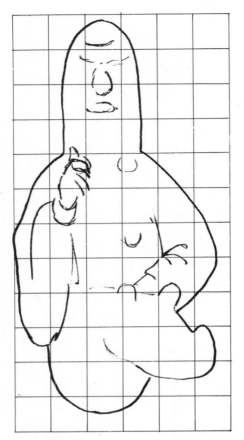

Figure 167

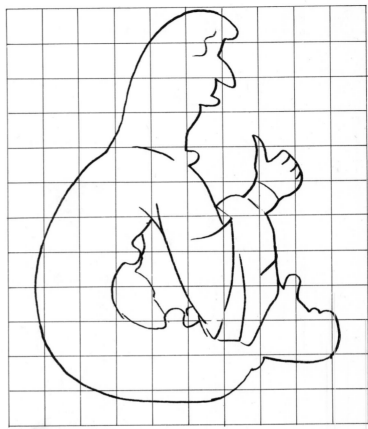

Figure 168

THIS is a fairly simple example of a constructed carving, that is to say it is built up from components rather than cut out of a single block. Some people object to this method although it is completely traditional, whereas carving everything from a large block tends rather to be a 20th century innovation.

The caterpillar is a character from Alice in Wonderland, who sits on a toadstool smoking a hookah pipe which, judging from the obscure comments he makes, may well be full of opium. He is a sour, bad-tempered person, and since in the Tenniel drawing he virtually has his back to us, I felt a sour, "drug addict" type of face would be appropriate.

The wood for the caterpillar was English boxwood, the mushrooms, walnut, and the base, burr elm.

In Fig. 171 the block of boxwood has been bandsawn from two sides but left attached to the waste end of the block by a small area at the bottom of the curve of his body, where he will eventually sit. Alternatively, he would be cut out completely and held with a carver's screw. The waste has been screwed to a larger block for holding in the bench vice.

In the picture the tail end of the cater-

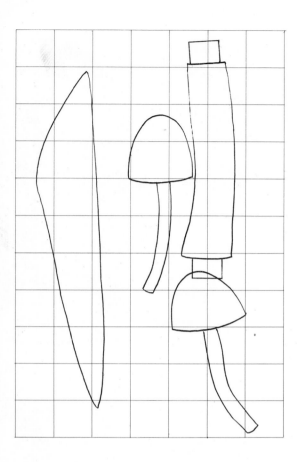

Figure 169

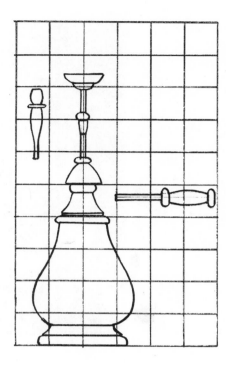

Figure 170

Figure 171   **Figure 172**

pillar's body can be seen on the nearside corner and the waste area on the left is marked for removal. Also the surplus extension of the left arm and the area between the arm and the body is indicated. The body lies diagonally across the block so the waste on its right side lies mostly towards the back. This can be seen on Fig. 172 on the left hand side. This right side here shows the arm holding the pipe and the area to be removed behind it. All this can be achieved by using a ¼″ (6mm) No. 9 and ¼″ (6mm) No. 3. Smaller tools are advisable on boxwood because of its hardness.

Figure 173

Figure 174

Figure 175

Figure 176

Figure 177

Figure 178

In Fig. 173 these areas of waste have been cut away and the shape of the figure is beginning to emerge. The arms can now be seen in their true perspective; the position of some of the legs is defined and the area between the arms and the inner curve of the body is apparent. Removing this area and carving the legs and hand within the hollow, in fact constitutes the bulk of the difficulty in creating this figure. Fig. 174 should help to clarify the shape of the body and how the waste can be removed by cutting under the arm. Still using the same chisels, begin cutting away the waste wood in the hollow of the body, from the front remembering that the legs must be left.

In Fig. 175 this has been started. Then attack from the left hand side cutting through under the arm and carefully leaving the shapes of the legs, Fig. 176. Having achieved this, very difficult and careful tooling and cleaning up of the forms in this area is necessary. The tiny scrapers and cutters used by dentists, work well on hardwoods such as box, and can be used to good effect in this area. A general shaping of the body and limbs can now proceed Figs. 177 and 178. Boxwood is, in my opinion, incomparable for this kind of work and should give no problems; tool work should be clean and precise and detailed to any degree you require.

Figure 179

Fig. 179 shows the right side with the left hand and the face partly shaped. We are getting down to the real detail now, and small tools are required, ⅛″ (3mm) No. 2 and, ⅛″ (3mm) No. 5. Obviously, your own hand holding a chisel is the perfect model for the caterpillar's holding his pipe. The left hand is resting on the body and can hardly be seen. Only the back of the hand needs carving, and although it is in an awkward spot, it presents no great difficulty.

Fig. 180 shows sketches of the right and left hands.

The face presents a problem, not so much in carving as in decision making. To say it will make or break the carving might be a little extreme, but if the face is wrong then certainly the whole subject of the study is going to lose its point. However the world is full of faces, and al-

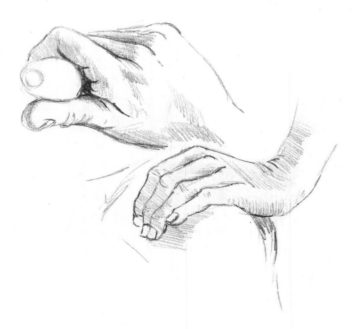

Figure 180

Figure 181

Figure 182

Figure 183

though it is a subjective judgement, there are accepted types as, I'm sure, any casting director would tell you. Fig 181 is the way I see the character described in the book.

Fig. 182 shows the hand nearing completion and the ridges in the back cut in. Also I have begun to file smooth the drapery on the arm. Fig. 183 shows the initial smoothing nearly complete. Rifler files are essential and it is a painstaking job. Also a ⅛″ (3mm) hole has been drilled in the hand to accept the pipe.

Figure 184

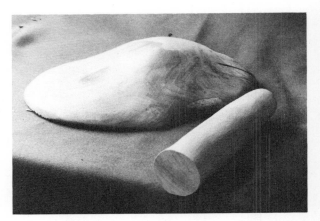

Figure 185

turned on the lathe (they could be carved similarly to the first one) and subsequently sanded on the drum to make them less symmetrical on the outside, Fig. 186. Cut in the familiar cracking that takes place with mushrooms, using, if necessary, a real mushroom as a model.

Figure 186

Fig. 184, the top of the large mushroom, made from walnut, has been bandsawn to an irregular circle and hollowed out with ½″ (12mm) No. 5. It has then been sanded smooth with a drum sander held in an electric drill. Drill a 1″ (25mm) hole in the centre to accept the end of the stem. Then, on one of the rare occasions when a V tool is ideal, cut the lines of the gills radiating from the centre. Having completed this, the mushroom can be turned over, screwed to a block from below into the centre hole, and the upper surface shaped and sanded. The stem was a roughly carved tapering cylinder and sanded on a drum, Fig. 185. The stems of the smaller mushrooms were made by the same method, but the tops were

Figure 187

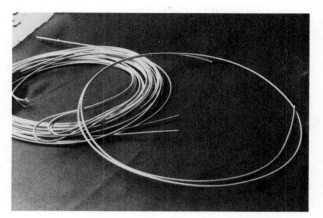

Figure 188

Figure 189

The hookah pipe and its small attachments, Fig. 187 and 188 were also turned on the lathe from boxwood, and an ⅛″ (3mm) hole drilled in the pipe attached to the hookah to accept the tube. This was made from cane of the type used to make small baskets, etc., and easily obtained in different thicknesses from craft supply shops. The cane was soaked in water and eventually glued into position.

Having sanded and polished the individual components, the parts were assembled and glued into position on a piece of elm burr which had had the bark removed, Fig. 189. Careful positioning of the caterpillar and hookah on the mushroom is necessary to ensure that they appear stable. A flat area was made for the hookah and a depression for the caterpillar and a steel dowel inserted for extra strength.

TWC–I

Tools used for this project	Timber:
	Boxwood (caterpillar)
	3″×6″×4½″
⅛″ (3mm) No. 2 gouge	(76mm×152mm×115mm)
⅛″ (3mm) No. 5 gouge	
¼″ (6mm) No. 9 gouge	Boxwood (hookah)
¼″ (6mm) No. 3 gouge	4½″×1½″×1½″
	(115mm×39mm×39mm)
Bench vice	
⅛″ (3mm) drill	1½″×½″×½″
Dental scrapers	(39mm×12mm×12mm)
Rifler files	
Abrasives	1¼″×½″×½″
	(32mm×12mm×12mm)

(continued p.130)

(continued from p.129)

Walnut (large mushroom top)
9″×9″×2″
(229mm×229mm×51mm)

Walnut (large mushroom stem)
7″×2″×2″
(178mm×51mm×51mm)

Walnut (small mushroom top)
5″×2″×2″
(127mm×51mm×51mm)

Walnut (small mushroom stem)
5″×2″×2″
(127mm×51mm×51mm)

Burr elm (base)
10″×10″×2″
(254mm×254mm×51mm)

Time: 5 days

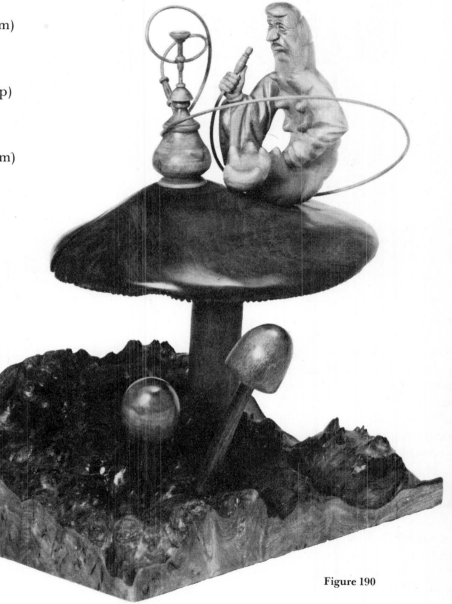

Figure 190

16 Horse

Figure 191

TO UNDERTAKE the carving of a horse at anything more than a superficial level is no small undertaking. Only dedicated and painstaking study of the animal in the preparatory stages will give a satisfying result at the finish.

A good start would be to watch the racing on the television and observe what appear to be elegant, highly-strung creatures that strut around the parade ring, shimmering in the sun. Then go to the races and see the real thing—great powerful beasts hot and sweating. Feel the ground shake under your feet as they thunder past at 30mph or so, throwing up great clods of earth. Watch the hunters plodding through the muddy ploughed fields in winter, mile after mile, and compare them to the great soft beasts with velvety noses and liquid eyes that inhabit riding school stables. You are, hopefully, absorbing in your mind something of the 'horsiness' of the horse without which your sculpture will be what a dressmaker's dummy is to a human being.

To carve anything in the round, you must have a total knowledge of its surface form. You cannot guess at what shape the other side may be, and since the horse is

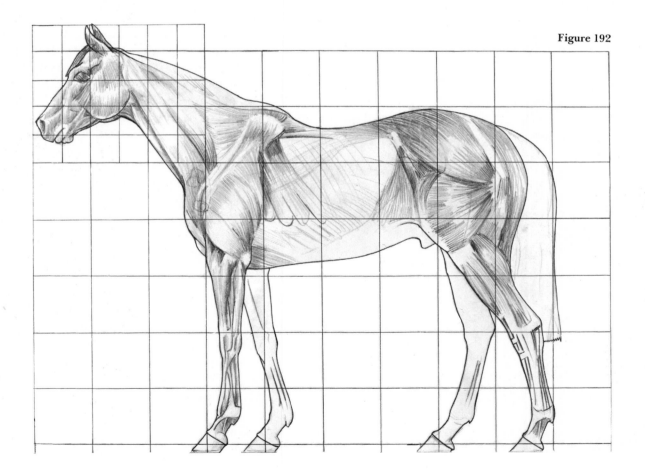

Figure 192

unlikely to stand still while you hack away at a block of wood, it is essential that a general understanding of the animal's physique is acquired.

First catch your horse, there are plenty about. Look at the horse from every possible angle, particularly from above, the side you are least familiar with. Familiarize yourself with its proportions and structure, the relationship between various parts, the action of the muscles, the soft bits and bony bits. Draw it, photograph it, read about it, look at other models and study its anatomy. Finally make a decision about the horse and what your carving will have to say about it.

Fig. 191 shows the original concept of the horse taken from a photograph of *Mill Reef* at stud. Every detail shown on the photograph is on the drawing. This may appear, and indeed is, an academic exercise, but at the end of drawing it you will know a little more about the horse than before.

Fig. 192 is a copy of the drawing, in which the musculature of the horse has been drawn. Make your first drawing (as Fig. 191) on tracing paper, then place it over the second drawing (Fig. 192) to get the muscular effect coming through. There is no reason why this process should not be carried out on the front view, back view and both sides. Sketches and studies of horses should be made, and some examples are shown in Fig. 193. When your knowledge of the subject is thorough, you will be able to exaggerate a detail here, diminish a form there, as required.

The timber for the horse illustrated was Brazilian mahogany from a local builders' merchant; not the best carving wood but certainly good enough, given sharp tools. The block required was 18″× 16×5½″ (457mm×406mm×140mm) and this was made up by gluing together two pieces of 3″ (76mm) board. It is essential that the joint is perfect, and the grain matching, since the glue-line will run

Figure 193

diagonally down one side of the face if the head is turned off-centre, this point cannot be over-emphasised. The main part of the glue-line should be arranged to run precisely down the centre of the horse, giving it maximum concealment. Since my horse has its head turned to one side, the block needs to be 5½" (140mm) thick, but if its neck is straightened out, this dimension can be reduced to about 3½" (90mm), possibly eliminating the need for a joint.

The grain and colour of mahogany are well suited to a carving of this type and size, when a fair amount of detail is required. A pronounced grain pattern tends to confuse the shape and make the form difficult to read. Limewood, pear, beech, and perhaps teak, would also be fine but I am well aware that availability and costs are often the over-riding considerations. However, bear in mind that you will spend many long hours making the piece and it would be a great shame to have to make excuses for the finished article, because the wood was uncarvable or faulty in some way.

Bandsaw the block of wood, leaving the spaces between the two front legs and two back legs for strength, Fig. 194. The front and back top profiles of the horse can now be drawn on the figure. Fig. 195 and Fig. 196.

Figure 194

Figure 195

Figure 196

Figure 197

Figure 198

Figure 199

Figure 200

Clamp the carving to the bench using a holdfast or G—cramp and cut away the large areas of waste on the sides using a ¾″ (19mm) No. 9, smoothing off with a ¾″ (19mm) No. 7. Fig. 197. This results in something like Fig. 198 and Fig. 199. The waste on the inside neck is marked, as are the areas round the legs. These can now be partly chopped away. The carving should now be screwed to a board into the feet, and the board held in the bench vice.

It is now that you need to study your drawings and photographs and live horses.

Your carving needs to be rounded-off—the smooth curves of the hind quarters and belly, the bunched muscles and bones of the limbs and the more angular details of the head. It cannot be over-stated that only reference to the horse itself can provide the information you require. I use a ½″ (12mm) No. 9 and a ¾″ (19mm) No. 5 for these stages and,

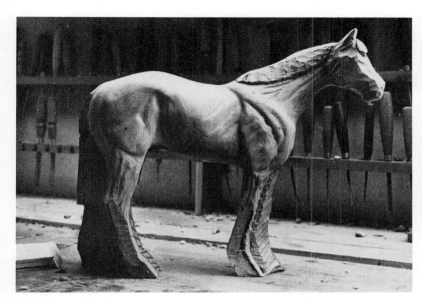

Figure 201

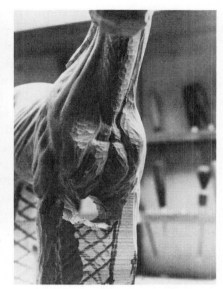

Figure 202

when the shape is beginning to look right, I smooth down with flat gouges ½″ (12mm) No. 2. This should result in something like Fig. 200. More detailed area of muscle can now be cut in, as well as details such as the mane, eyes, nostrils, jaw bones, and so on. These are cut in with a small gouge ¼″ (6mm) No. 9, or ⅛″ (3mm) V tool and blended in. Shape around the legs until the web between them is almost broken through and cut-in round the tail and under the belly. Smooth down as in Fig. 201, up to this stage.

Work the more detailed areas of muscle round the front (Fig. 202), and back of the horse, and under the belly as far as possible. Now remove the figure from the board and hold it upside down in the vice, suitably padded, and cut away the waste between the legs completely, putting in the details under the belly and tail. It is as well to finish these

areas completely at this stage, thereby eliminating the need to remove the board again. Having re-fixed the horse to the board, smooth the whole figure with files down to the feet, in order to see what you have achieved so far, Fig. 203.

Figure 203

We must now consider the finer points of the horse. Very accurate measurements must be taken to ensure equal sizes of hooves, limbs, eyes, ears, etc. Remember that a lump or distortion in the wrong place, that may be just a slip of the chisel to you, may indicate a crippling disease to someone who knows about horses. Whilst we are not trying to produce a slavish facsimile of the animal, it would be ludicrous if it had the equivalent of a club foot or hunched back.

The finishing stage of the carving is a process of refining, paring down the muscles and bones to more and more accurate detail until a satisfactory level is reached. Particular attention must be paid to the head, which should now appear as Fig. 204. Reference to the earlier project on the pony's head should resolve this problem.

You may wish to include veins, eyelids, and tiny variations of surface caused by tense sinews or muscles; or a more approximate treatment of surfaces and planes might be preferable. For instance, I felt that, in view of the large area of smooth polished wood of the body, I would provide a contrast by texturing the hair of the mane and tail with a V-tool. Bear in mind, if you do this, that it is wise to start the cuts with the side of the V-tool that is cutting against the grain on the waste side, so that the wood which is weakened by the previous cut has least strain on it. Nothing looks worse than hair that appears to be crumbling away.

Figure 204

The final stage in the carving is the finishing process. If you decide on a tooled finish, then very sharp edges are required and a wide range of gouges in order to achieve a smooth, clean cut on every shape and surface. It is a long difficult process.

A smooth sanded finish takes even longer. Use good quality paper—preferably an aluminium oxide—starting with medium grit on the larger planes and finer, say 120 grit, on the more detailed areas. It is obviously vital that details are not worn away, so small rifler files and folded abrasive paper must be carefully used. Self-adhesive sanding sheets can be applied to shaped pieces of wood to good effect.

When you feel you have produced an immaculate surface over every square inch, it is wise, at this level of work to leave the carving for a few days. After hours of tedious sanding it is easy to say 'that is good enough' but when some time has elapsed you may reconsider your decision. If you can prevail on someone qualified, to give it a final going over, so much the better, and it is wise to dip the piece in water to raise the grain and rub down yet again. This is really essential if you are to stain the wood.

I stained my horse with a brownish mahogany spirit stain and, while it was still wet, I slightly blackened the legs, tail, mane and nose, typical of a bay horse. I then gave it two coats of brown shellac sealer, which I again carefully sanded. Several good coats of wax polish later, it was finished. The sanding and polishing took about three full working days. Still, after all this cleaning up, there are distinct toolcuts and a sliver of grain mising which are really quite irritating and impossible to remove without completely ruining the staining.

The finished horse was screwed through the hooves to a block of burr oak, which I left unstained with just a wax polish finish. Fig. 205.

Tools used
for this project:—

¾″ (19mm) No. 9 gouge	¼″ (6mm) No. 2 gouge
¾″ (19mm) No. 7 gouge	⅛″ (3mm) No. 2 gouge
½″ (12mm) No. 9 gouge	⅛″ (3mm) No. 9 gouge
¾″ (19mm) No. 5 gouge	¼″ (6mm) No. 3 gouge
⅛″ (3mm) V chisel	¼″ (6mm) No. 9 gouge
½″ (12mm) No. 2 gouge	

Bench vice	Timber: Mahogany
Files	18″×16″×5½″
Rifler Files	(457mm×406mm×140mm)
Abrasives	
Holdfast and G-clamp	
Ukibori punches	Time: 7 days

Figure 205

17 Falstaff

Figure 206

NOTHING has inspired more works of art of all kinds than the human form and character, and none more fascinating than the characters created by Shakespeare.

There are no definitive illustrations to Shakespeare but a thorough study of a particular personality will soon evolve an image. Sir John Falstaff is one of the most vivid portrayals and justifiably one of the most popular. Only a few clues are given about his appearance: he is large and fat, old, and has a white beard; but his characteristics are clearly revealed. He drinks and eats to excess, he lies, cheats and steals and is not averse to the ladies. His cowardice seems based on the premise that bravery is not worth the candle. Despite these unlikeable habits he comes over more as a lecherous old rogue than a criminal.

I don't see costume as an important issue. Shakespeare's plays are frequently out of period in details and have been performed in all manner of dress. In fact,

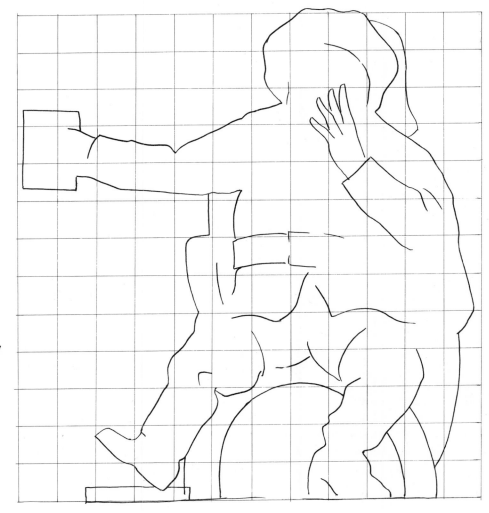

Figure 207

Figure 208

Falstaff can be anything you want him to be within the limitations stated.

My first step in carving an imaginary figure is to find a real one to act as a model. To this end I recruited a friend, padded him out a bit and dressed him in an old, belted leather jacket and a pair of boots. My first drawings were taken from him to establish the pose I liked. The face is purely imaginary, as is the hat and cloak, although the folds of all the clothes are taken from samples of the appropriate fabrics.

The next stage is to translate a preliminary sketch into an accurate full size working drawing of a front and side view. This does not have to be complete in every detail but it is the ground plan for your carving. It will be transferred to the faces of your wood and be bandsawn. Any alterations or variations must really be within the framework of this plan. An excellent carving wood to use for this project is limewood. It has extremely good detail-cutting properties and is freely available in reasonable sizes. The colour, in this case, matters only in that the intention is to stain it to an antique gold brown. I cannot see Falstaff as something new and clean—he must have an oldness about him.

The block I used was 8″×10″ and about 15″ long (204mm×254mm×382mm), part of some baulks cut twelve years ago, and in my workshop for about four; it has remained virtually flawless despite having the heart running down it. I would

still need to glue on an extra piece for half an arm and a foot but these could be left till later.

Having traced the profiles onto the wood with carbon paper the block is bandsawn from both sides and securely screwed to the bench top. The piece now appears as in Fig. 209. The main lines are drawn on the wood in felt tip and large areas to be removed are hatched. It is very important, I feel, to study the figure carefully and get it clear in your mind exactly the shape and position of the piece of wood to be removed. Try to visualise them as a section of a plaster mould round a casting. Having established this in your mind's eye, using the

Figure 209

Figure 210

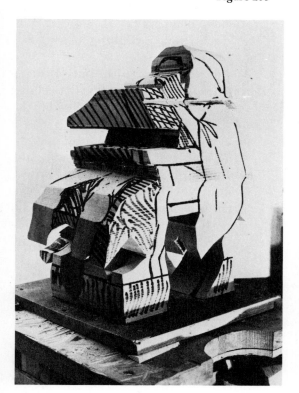

Figure 211

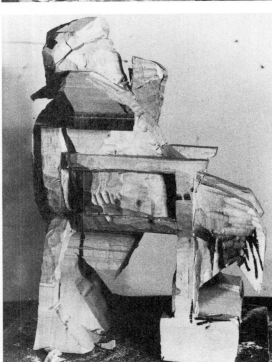

Figure 212

largest suitable tool, remove the waste as efficiently as possible. It is hopeless to whittle away at the block hoping that the right shape will appear. It won't. You must know where the shape is and uncover it. The only way to gain this knowledge is by constant study of your drawings and a real human being. Spatial relationships are almost impossible to grasp without something concrete to refer to.

Fig. 210 and 211, show the area between the legs, between the chair arms and the extension of the right hand removed. The waste is marked on the back of the head around the feathers, the shape of the cloak on the back of the chair and the general shape of the chair frame.

Fig 212 shows these areas removed, and now some shaping of the forms can begin. This is fairly straight forward if the main areas have been accurately located. You should soon have something looking like Fig. 213.

At this point I begin to put in more detailed features and I start with the head because I can easily relate the head to the other parts of the body and use it as a scale of measurement. The head must be detailed and full of character and life. The lines in the hair were put in with a ⅛″ (3mm) No. 11. Recessing the eyes was assisted by a 1/16″ (1.5mm) straight dental burr in a flexi-shaft. The left hand followed, using my left hand as a model, Fig. 214.

Make your own rough sketches to determine detail at each stage. An example is shown in Fig. 215.

Follow the left arm down the sleeve and on to the cloak at the side and back, Fig. 216. I used a leather jacket as a model for the sleeve, and cotton table-cloth for the cloak. I like to think that something of the nature of different materials will come through in the carving. After the cloak, the front of the body and legs can be completed. The chair can be finished at the same time. File and glass-paper the carving as it is being completed, piece by piece so that you can see what the finished carving will be like.

Use rotary burrs for difficult under-cutting and for delicate areas which might easily be broken using gouges, and use them for the lace effect on the collar.

Having completed the figure down to the left foot the block for the right leg can be glued on. This is always a tricky business and with my carving I was rather disappointed in this instance. When the

Figure 213

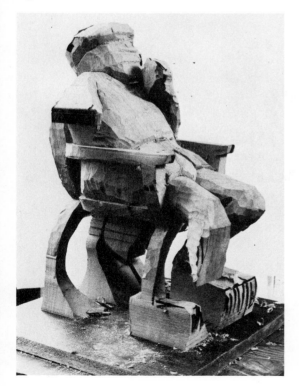

Figure 214

carving was finally oiled, the areas immediately adjacent to the glue-line showed a distinct discolouration caused by the PVA glue being absorbed into the surfaces. This can be eliminated by the use of epoxy resin. The joint on the arm was much better.

The carving of the leg is fairly straight forward, make the folds of the leather boots as deep and narrow as possible around the ankle and knee joint — shallow carving is never very satisfactory. Because of the stress factors involved when working on the extended leg work your way up from the toe in order that most strain should be on it while the upper parts are still strong, Fig. 217.

Lace collars
— Rembrandt.

Figure 215

Figure 216

At this point carve the chair with some simple chip carving to make the surface less plain. It is best finished before the arm is fixed on as this will get in the way. It could also have been done before gluing on the leg.

The feathers on the hat, Fig. 218, are not easy and you may find that under-cutting them, even with the help of rotary burrs, is most difficult. It would probably be more successfully accomplished if the feathers are carved separately and applied. Similar consideration might be given to the tankard in the right hand. It could easily be turned on the lathe, the handle applied and the whole set into a

Figure 217

Figure 218

suitably carved hand. It is a question, not of rights and wrongs, but aesthetic judgement. A turned tankard set into the hand looks exactly that, and as the only separate piece, I feel it would not sit well on the carving. If on the other hand Falstaff also carried a separately made sword, dagger, turned buttons, spurs etc., they would blend together, but the whole carving would then take on a different visual impact.

The right arm in the carving was carved up to the end of the stump prior to fixing on the block for the forearm. This was dowelled and glued with epoxy resin, since it was almost impossible to apply any pressure other than by hand. The arm will need support for some of the heavier cutting and this can be done by the hand as in Fig. 219. There is no doubt that there are dangers to one's self with this method of working and only

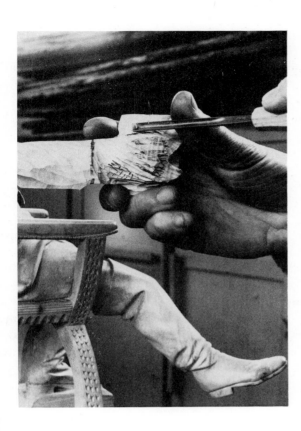

Figure 219

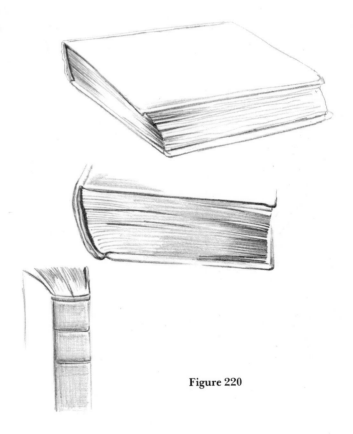

Figure 220

experienced carvers should attempt it. Some measure of protection is possible by using a heavy leather glove but there would be a definite loss of sensitivity and thus a lack of control. There is no substitute for experience and concentration.

The book under the outstretched foot is made separately and its function is as a title for the carving. An old leather-bound volume was used as a model, and if such a book is studied it will be seen that the pages tend to divide themselves into the separate bound sections, Fig. 220. Admittedly, the pressure of a foot on the book would probably tend to close these divisions, but it is the carver's prerogative to ignore such details if he chooses. The division of the pages was cut with a V tool and the splits at the corners sawn out with a fine modeller's saw. Notice the gap between the binding of the spine and the sewn pages. The title of the carving is cut on the front in script using a V tool.

The whole is set on a block of brown oak carved to resemble flagstones and finally darkened and oiled. Fig. 221.

Anyone who makes something knows every fault in it. I am certainly never 100% happy with a carving and Falstaff is no exception. But I do feel I have captured something of the character I envisaged—a dissolute, lecherous old man expounding some bawdy exploit of dubious authenticity to a crony in the tavern. If something of that communicates itself to the onlooker, then I feel that the carving is worth the effort.

It is difficult to define the satisfaction to be gained from creating an object—I hesitate to use the expression "work of art" because I don't believe it has to be one—but I think that, whilst the fulfilment of having struggled with the problems of woodcarving and at least partially succeeded may be an end in itself, there is no doubt that approval from a qualified audience is a more lasting and positive uplift. Objective criticism is rare amongst friends and it is wise to seek out the opinions of those who understand the subject. It will be invaluable to your work.

Above all, make every carving special, as if the world would judge you by that alone, and you can be sure that your efforts will not go unnoticed.

Tools used for this project
⅛″ (3mm) No. 9 gouge
½″ (12mm) No. 9 gouge
¼″ (6mm) No. 9 gouge
¼″ (6mm) No. 2 gouge
½″ (12mm) No. 2 gouge
⅛″ (3mm) No. 2 gouge
¼″ (6mm) 'V' chisel
⅛″ (3mm) No. 11 gouge

Flexi-shaft & burrs
Rifler files

Abrasives
Modeller's saw

Timber: Limewood
8″×10″×15″
(204mm×254mm×382mm)

Brown oak
15″×12″×2″
(382mm×305mm×51mm)

Time: 15 days

Figure 221

Bibliography

THE CARVER'S COMPANION	P. Martin	A. & C. Black	1958
WOODCARVING	P. Hasluck, Editor	Cassell & Co.	1958
CARVING & DESIGN	L. Miller	Pitman	1936
SCULPTURE IN WOOD	P. E. Norman	Studio	1954
A MANUAL OF WOODCARVING	W. Bemrose	Bemrose & Son	1906
LIMEWOOD CARVERS OF RENAISSANCE GERMANY	M. Baxandall	Yale University	1980
DECORATIVE WOODWORK	Grimwood & Goodyear	University of London	1936
LIVING ANATOMY	R. D. Lockhart	Faber & Faber	1949
PRACTICAL WOODCARVING	E. Rowe	Batsford	1930
PRACTICAL WOODCARVING & GILDING	W. Wheeler & C. Hayward	Evans Bros.	1973
WOODCARVING	C. G. Leland	Pitman	1931
WHITTLING & WOODCARVING	E. J. Tangerman	McGraw-Hill	1936
CONCISE HISTORY OF MODERN SCULPTURE	H. Read	Thames & Hudson	1971
HERALDIC SCULPTURE	J. Woodford	Benham	1973
ENKU	G. F. Dotzenko	Kodansha International	1976
MASTERS OF WOOD SCULPTURE	N. Roukes	Pitman	1980
THE ART OF NETSUKE CARVING	Masatoshi, Bushell	Kodansha International	1981
GRINLING GIBBONS	H. Avray Tipping	Country Life	1914

Index